MW01419323

Gratitude On The Prairie

Cycle B Sermons for Proper 18 – Thanksgiving
Based on the Gospel Texts

Thomas C. Willadsen

CSS Publishing Company, Inc.

Lima, Ohio

Gratitude On The Prairie

FIRST EDITION

Library of Congress Cataloging-in-Publication Data:

Names: Willadsen, Thomas C., author. Title: Gratitude on the prairie : cycle B sermons for Proper 18-Thanksgiving based on the gospel texts / Thomas C. Willadsen. Description: First edition. | Lima, Ohio : CSS Publishing Company, Inc., 2020. | Identifiers: LCCN 2020026693 | ISBN 9780788029998 (paperback) | ISBN 9780788030000 (ebook) Subjects: LCSH: Bible. Gospels--Sermons. | Bilbe--Sermons. | Common lectionary (1992). | Church year sermons. Classification: LCC BS2555.54 .W55 2020 | DDC 252/.6--dc23 LC record available at https://lccn.loc.gov/2020026693

For more information about CSS Publishing Company resources, visit our website at www.csspub.com, email us at csr@csspub.com, or call (800) 241-4056.

e-book:
ISBN-13: 978-0-7880-3000-0
ISBN-10: 0-7880-3000-0

ISBN-13: 978-0-7880-2999-8
ISBN-10: 0-7880-2999-1

DIGITALLY PRINTED

My sermons always grow out of conversations with the congregations I serve as well as with friends and colleagues. I have been richly blessed by their support, encouragement, feedback, disagreement, and observations for the past thirty plus years:

- Westminster Presbyterian, Peoria, Illinois, my home congregation;
- The Northwestern University Marching Band, (NUMB), where I learned that leading acts of public silliness really was good preparation for parish ministry;
- Lincoln Park and Ravenswood Presbyterian Churches, Chicago, where I served during and just after seminary;
- First Presbyterian Church, Mankato, Minnesota, my first call;
- Towson Presbyterian Church, Baltimore, Maryland, my second call;
- First Presbyterian Church, Oshkosh, Wisconsin, my first solo call; and
- Faith Presbyterian Church, La Vista, Nebraska, where I now serve as transitional pastor.

To the great cloud of pastors I have come to know, I thank you for answering, "Absolutely!" when asked, "Will you be a friend among your colleagues in ministry?"

Contents

Did Jesus Say What I Think He Said? *7*

Proper 18 / Ordinary Time 23 / Pentecost 15
Isaiah 35:4-7a; Psalm 146; James 2:1-10, (11-13), 14-17; and Mark 7:24-37

The Power Of Weakness ***12***

Proper 19 / Ordinary Time 24 / Pentecost 16
Psalm 19; Mark 8:27-38

Repetition, Repetition, Repetition ***17***

Proper 20 / Ordinary Time 25 / Pentecost 17
Proverbs 31:10-31; Psalm 1, Mark 9:30-37

It's Lonely At The Top ***22***

Proper 21 / Ordinary Time 26 / Pentecost 18
Esther 7:1-6, 9-10, 9:20-22; Psalm 124; Mark 9:38-50; Numbers 11:4-6, 10-16, 24-29

What's In A Name? ***26***

Proper 22 / Ordinary Time 27 / Pentecost 19
Psalm 8; Hebrews 1:1-4, 2:5-12; Mark 10:2-16

Recush רכוש ***32***

Proper 23 / Ordinary Time 28 / Pentecost 20
Psalm 90:12-17; Hebrews 4:12-16; Mark 10:17-31

Baptized In Water ***36***

Proper 24 / Ordinary Time 29 / Pentecost 21
Psalm 104:1-9, 24, 35c; Mark 10:35-45

Seeing With The Eyes Of Faith ***40***

Proper 25 / Ordinary Time 30 / Pentecost 22
Psalm 34:1-8, (19-22); Jeremiah 31:7-9; Psalm 126; Mark 10:46-52

Bread For The Journey ***46***

Proper 26 / Ordinary Time 31 / Pentecost 23
Ruth 1:1-18; Psalm 146; Deuteronomy 6:1-9; Psalm 119:1-8;
Hebrews 9:11-14; Mark 12:28-34

The Rhythm Of The Saints ***52***

All Saints' Day
John 11:32-44; Isaiah 25:6-9; Revelation 21:1-6a; Psalm 24

Good News From The Threshing Floor ***56***

Proper 27 / Ordinary Time 32 / Pentecost 24
Ruth 3:1-5; 4,13-17; Psalm 146; Mark 12:38-44

Steadfast Change ***60***

Proper 28 / Ordinary Time 33 / Pentecost 25
1 Samuel 1:4-20; 1 Samuel 2:1-10; Hebrews 10:11-14, (15-18), 19-25;
Mark 13:1-8

Christ, Our King ***66***

Reign Of Christ / Ordinary Time 34 / Pentecost 26
2 Samuel 23:1-7; Psalm 132:1-12, (13-18); Daniel 7:9-10, 13-14;
Psalm 93; Revelation 1:4b-8; John 18:33-37

Gratitude On The Prairie ***72***

Thanksgiving Day
Joel 2:21-27; Psalm 126; Matthew 6:25-33

Proper 18 / Ordinary Time 23 / Pentecost 15

Isaiah 35:4-7a; Psalm 146; James 2:1-10, (11-13), 14-17;
Mark 7:24-37

Did Jesus Say What I Think He Said?

This morning's gospel lesson may be the most troubling passage in the gospels because Jesus said a lot of provocative things to the religious authorities. The crowds were delighted with the clever ways he always seemed to best them in battles of wits. This morning's gospel passage is different — very different.

Jesus and his disciples needed a break. Just before today's passage begins, Jesus had a controversy with some Pharisees. It appears that the Pharisees had traveled from Jerusalem to Gennesaret because they heard that his disciples did not wash their hands properly. We know the Pharisees were fanatics about this sort of thing, what we often overlook is the lengths the Pharisees would go to prove that they were righteous, blameless, innocent, and others, in a word, weren't. In this case the length they went to was *ninety miles*. Let that sink in. A committee of leaders of the temple traveled, over land, ninety miles to point out someone else's error. What do you take so seriously that you're willing to walk for a whole week or more ? In fairness to the Pharisees, they may have ridden donkeys or maybe even camels. What would you endure several days' worth of saddle sores to do?

In the ensuing battle of wits, Jesus showed several ways the Pharisees were hypocrites, and he delighted the crowd who had come to observe the contest. He even went on to say that what one puts into one's body is nowhere near as important as what comes out of people's hearts. Here Mark interjected that in making this statement, Jesus declared all foods clean. Anyway, it appears that the debate had wearied Jesus, so he and the disciples left town and went into the region of Tyre. Tyre is a city on the Mediterranean, about fifty miles from Gennesaret, where Jesus had his conversation with the Pharisees. Jesus was putting some serious distance between him and the site of his most recent discussion. He was probably weary, if not from the Pharisees, certainly from the fifty-mile trip. He wanted to lie low, to escape notice. It didn't work.

The gospel lesson begins with Jesus' desire to get away from his adoring fans. (I always imagine scenes from the Beatles' "Hard Day's Night" when I picture the throngs hounding Jesus at every moment.) The woman who approached Jesus was not a Jew; she was a resident of the coastal area where Jesus and his disciples had gone. This is one of very few places where there is an actual dialogue between Jesus and someone else. There's the woman at the well in John's gospel and something like dialogue during Jesus' "trial," but in this passage there's something like banter, or if looked at properly, it is banter. I'll explain what I mean by "looked at properly."

On its face, Jesus' response to the woman appeared to be like a snippy waitress who snapped, "Not my table," to guests at a restaurant waiting for service. The waitress *could* serve the guests but for some reason not visible to the guests, she chose not to.

Is this something you would expect from your Lord and Savior, how he responded to a woman who had knelt before him, begging for her daughter's deliverance from demonic possession? Jesus appeared icily aloof. Or maybe he was still weary from his run-in with the Pharisees. He told the woman that his mission was to "feed" the lost children of Israel, his people. To give her attention, while neglecting them would be like taking food off the children's table and giving it to dogs. Scholars debate whether the Greek word Jesus used is closer to "puppies" than "dogs," no matter the precise term, it is offensive. It does not stretch the text at all to say that Jesus practically called the woman a "B word." And that would have been every bit as offensive in the original setting as it would be in ours. What can we make of this Jesus? The Jesus in this passage who heard of a need for healing, yet who declined to respond?

Sit with that question for a while, as we look at this morning's other readings. The psalm says:

The Lord lifts up those who are bowed down;
The Lord loves the righteous.
The Lord watches over the strangers;
he upholds the orphan and the widow....

That sounds a lot like a certain woman from Syro-Phoenician woman we just heard about. If the Lord lifts, loves, watches over, and upholds the vulnerable, what did Jesus think he was doing?

Then there was James, possibly Jesus' biological brother, who wrote this:

My brothers and sisters, do you with your acts of favoritism really believe in our glorious Lord Jesus Christ? For if a person with gold rings and in fine clothes comes into your assembly, and if a poor person in dirty clothes also comes in, and if you take notice of the one wearing the fine clothes and say, "Have a seat here, please," while to the one who is poor you say, "Stand there," or, "Sit at my feet," have you not made distinctions among yourselves, and become judges with evil thoughts? Listen, my beloved brothers and sisters. Has not God chosen the poor in the world to be rich in faith and to be heirs of the kingdom that he has promised to those who love him? But you have dishonored the poor. Is it not the rich who oppress you? Is it not they who drag you into court? Is it not they who blaspheme the excellent name that was invoked over you?
You do well if you really fulfill the royal law according to the scripture, "You shall love your neighbor as yourself." But if you show partiality, you commit sin and are convicted by the law as transgressors.

James 2:1-9, (NRSV).

What would the conversation around the dinner table be that night after Jesus insulted a woman of a different ethnic group? Do you think James would get on his brother's case for showing partiality? By James' logic, Jesus had convicted himself. *Hmm, maybe Jesus was out of line when he talked to that lady...."*

Then there's this choice bit from the prophet Isaiah:

Then the eyes of the blind shall be opened,and the ears of the deaf unstopped;then the lame shall leap like a deer,and the tongue of the speechless sing for joy.

Isaiah 35:5-6 (NRSV)

Jesus got around to making the deaf hear and giving speech to the mute in the second part of today's gospel reading.

The Lord looks out for widows and orphans; the faithful follower of Jesus shows no partiality and knows to love one's neighbor as oneself.... Yet, Jesus insulted a woman who had come to beg for her daughter's restoration.

We get the happy ending, the woman's daughter's demon was expelled from her body, so maybe we should just leave this scene alone and write it off as Jesus not being at his best because he was weary. Such a reading certainly supports the "fully human" side of his identity.

It may be that Jesus was defeated in this war of words. The woman — we never learn her name — out-bantered a guy who bantered pretty well. The Big Guy recognized he had been beaten and as a concession or out of respect — one banterer to another — he healed the daughter. Think about that for a minute; the Pharisees, the Sadducees, the scribes, the teachers, the priests, the religious authorities, they never out-foxed Jesus in a battle of wits. This kneeling, devoted mother must be pretty darn special. She won! You have to admire her strategy: rather than pushing back against being called a dog (or worse), she rolled with the insult and turned it back to Jesus. It was as though she was saying, "Jesus, treating me like a dog is just fine, it will be sufficient to heal my daughter; my faith tells me so."

So maybe Jesus' healing the daughter was his way of saying, something like, "Well played, worthy opponent!"

There's another lens through which to view this encounter, one that gives the woman her due, but also presented Jesus in a way that maintains our expectation of his kindness and openness. Elton Trueblood is the theologian who first exposed me to this idea. Trueblood believed that from the start, Jesus entered his encounter with the woman with a certain playfulness, an awareness that society's conventions would lead him to ignore or spurn the woman's request. Instead of making fun of the woman, he and she are making a statement about the culture in which they both lived which would expect, or even demand, Jesus keeping the woman at a distance. The difficulty here is we have to provide the twinkle in the woman's eye and the arch in Jesus' eyebrow, as together they subvert the cultural expectations that surround them.

Here's the best example I can give to a modern occurrence of this. My junior year in college, I had an internship that took me off campus Monday through Thursday between 8 am and 5 pm. I needed to drop a course and add a course, but the office where I needed to do that was not open on Friday. I was stuck. I went to the office anyway on a Friday morning, and explained the situation to the receptionist in the office. She hemmed a little, "Well, I don't know… I guess this once… you have an honest face…."

"You're not about to cut through the red tape for me, are you? That's either unprecedented, or it's never been done before!"

This entire dialogue was a way we could both see the silliness of the system that we both operated in. My response was even something like a compliment, as though I was saying, "You know, for a pencil pushing bureaucrat, you're not all bad." Our conversation could have gone terribly wrong — and I would not have been able to drop "Masterpieces of French Literature," if she had not conspired, wordlessly, with me to go off script and bend the rules. I had to promise that I'd read "*Madame Bovary*," but it was worth it.

Imagine Jesus and the woman having that kind of conversation. It shows a playful side to Jesus and the woman's willingness to play along makes the story all the richer.

Amen.

Proper 19 / Ordinary Time 24 / Pentecost 16

Psalm 19; Mark 8:27-38

The Power Of Weakness

Our lessons this morning feels like an archery target. The psalm starts with the long view, the perspective of the psalmist marveling at the beauty of creation.

"The heavens are telling the glory of God," it begins, but that translation doesn't quite capture the essence of what is to be expressed Psalm 19:1 (NRSV). It more closely means, "The heavens are continually telling the glory of God." It's always happening, without ceasing. All we have to do is look up, notice the beauty of the stars, feel the warmth of the sun, marvel at the shape of the clouds, and we are reminded of God's glory.

Next, the psalm does something surprising — after the majestic language about God as the Creator of the universe, the sustainer of heaven, the psalm devotes the next verses to praising God for the gift of the law — the gift of instruction Psalm 19:2 (NRSV). This kind of language in Psalms always sounds odd to me, as an American I treasure my freedom and independence, the idea that anyone would be grateful, or be moved to praise God for law seems strange to us. We all know laws restrict freedom. There was a bar down the street from my house in Wisconsin — there's a bar down *every* street — the bar I have in mind had a sign that says, "Rules just slow you down." That's how most of us look at laws, so the Hebrew appreciation, even love of law takes us by surprise.

And yet, there are moments when I am grateful, very grateful for clear, concise instructions. An unbreakable deadline, for example, is as much a gift as a burden. For example, Thursday is sermon writing day for me, and I know when Thursday starts exactly how much time

I have to devote to composing my sermon for Sunday. I've learned to do the best I can within those constraints. There is no possible way I could get an extension. Oh, I suppose I could ask the office staff to call all the members and friends of the church and say, "We're sorry, Tom won't have his sermon ready until Tuesday; we hope you can join us for worship at 9:30 am that day." The unbreakable deadline is a gift that sets me free. I'm free to have family time and sabbath time on Friday and Saturday because of the unbreakable deadline I set for myself on Thursday — and the even more rigid deadline that is Sunday morning.

The psalmist wrote of the teachings of the Lord found in scripture that they are sweeter than the drippings of the honeycomb and more desired than gold. Think about that! God's laws are something we can taste and something we can long for with our hearts, they are very personal and close to home.

The psalm goes from the beauty of the stars in the heavens, the majesty of creation, to the gift of God's law which we learn and internalize and concludes with a prayer that his words and thoughts will be acceptable to God (Psalm 19:3-4 NRSV).

The gospel lesson gets even closer to the bull's eye. Jesus drew his disciples into a conversation about his identity and their relationship to him. Again, he started with a wide circle, "Who do people say that I am?" and the answers the disciples give him are that he is thought of as a forerunner of the Messiah. But Peter said, "You are the Messiah." Mark 8:27-29 (NRSV). There's a huge difference between the one who has come before — the one who announces the coming of the Christ — and the Christ himself. And in just about every way, the Christ who is about to come, but is not yet here, is a lot easier to deal with! All we can do while we await Christ is to be ready. I saw a bumper sticker once that said, "Jesus is coming; look busy." And that's where the disciples were and where the rest of the people who thought of Jesus as a forerunner were.

But Peter identified that Jesus as the Christ, the Messiah — the one they had been waiting for, had arrived. And it's not what you'd expect, Jesus didn't say, "yes" or "no" to Peter. It said, "He sternly ordered them not to tell anyone about him." Mark 8:30 (NRSV). He went on then to explain that he would suffer terribly, be rejected by the religious authorities and killed, but rise again after three days. He was totally, transparently honest about this. In Mark's gospel there is no Messiah, no Christ, until after the crucifixion. Peter spoke for many of us, perhaps most of us, who want a relationship with Christ without the suffering, the agony, the betrayal, and the abandonment of the cross. Peter rebuked Jesus, resisting the ghastly reality that Jesus foretold. It's as though Peter said, "It can't be that way, Jesus. We won't let it be that way!" Remember later in the story it is Peter, who said he'd always be faithful, yet denied Jesus three times.

And Jesus' response was stunning: "Get behind me Satan!" Mark 8:33 (NRSV). This is the one disciple who ten seconds before had correctly identified him as the Messiah! Now this one, passionate disciple is called God's adversary — that's what "Satan" means. All because he can't or won't imagine that his friend would be tortured and killed. Jesus used the same language with Peter that he used in driving demons out of people. It's as though Peter's wrong notion of Jesus' identity is as crippling as demonic possession.

What does it say about Jesus' coming reign that someone so close to him could be so wrong about the path that lay ahead, the path that Jesus was called to walk? That the one who identified him as the long-promised Messiah would want to cling to him and not let him fulfill — actually try to keep him from fulfilling — God's plan through him?

Jesus told Peter and all those gathered around that there was no way into God's kingdom that bypassed the cross. That's not a happy message, it's not the basis for the feel good movie of the summer. But it's how God is alive and how God is at work redeeming each of us, all of us, and all of creation.

One prominent preacher said, "You cannot succeed preaching the cross. People do not want to hear it; they already have enough problems." (Fred B. Craddock, John Hayes & Carl Holladay, *Preaching Through the Christian Year: Year B* (Harrisburg, PA: Trinity Press International, 1993), 147). And at one level I think he's correct. What do we mean when we say, "We all have our crosses to bear?" You've said that; I've said it. We mean everyone's got problems. "You want to complain, go ahead, but you're not alone. In fact, if it's a contest, my problems are probably worse than yours!"

So, what was Jesus thinking trying to get people to follow him, denying themselves to follow him to the cross of suffering? Losing one's life to save it? Even rejoicing when we suffer for righteousness? Is anyone going to sign up for that?

It's easy to believe in God when we're alone, looking at the beauty of the sky as the psalmist described. It's even easy to be grateful to God for the gift of the instruction we find in the Bible. If we're studying alone and can smugly say to ourselves, "Think how wonderful the world would be if everyone obeyed God's word."

But faith in Christ calls us out of solitary pursuits. Faith in Christ call us to proclaim Christ where the hurt is the worst, where despair is the deepest, where hope has never been born. We can't sit under our telescope or at our desk and respond fully to Christ. We have to feel the brokenness around us. We have to be touched, even wounded by it.

I had a classmate in seminary who was in the midst of despair and found himself sitting in a church, sure that no one understood what he was going through. He struggled with painful moments of doubt and uncertainty. It was his dark night of the soul. The certain knowledge that he was failing, not just his classes, but also failing to live up to the expectations of his loved ones. As a man, as a student, as a future preacher of the Christian gospel, my friend was broken. He looked up and saw a crucifix — not a cross — a crucifix. A cross with Jesus' body hanging on it.

Presbyterians do not have crucifixes. We have crosses, empty crosses, because we emphasize the resurrection, not the torture of the crucifixion. We live on this side of the blood, nails, thorns, mocking, spitting, and abandonment.

No, my classmate was not in a Presbyterian church, nor was he Presbyterian. He looked up and saw a crucifix and said, "You *do* understand, God!" My classmate suddenly and in a life-changing way understood that God's love did not just include failures, but God's love embraces us, seeks us out, and regards us not as failures but as beloved children.

In 1989, 96 fans were crushed in a soccer stadium in Sheffield, England; another 200 were injured. At one of the hospitals to which victims were taken, an attending surgeon spoke to the parents who had come to find out the fate of their children. The surgeon read the names of those killed, expressed his sympathy to the parents, and then said that as a Christian he believed God understood the parents' grief and was with them in their time of need. One father bitterly responded: "What does God know about losing a son?" (Grant Keizer, "Grief and Grievance: The Tyrrany of the Dead" in *Christian Century* vol. 120, no. 10 (May 2003), 7).

This is what we need to remember: that the God of the earth and stars loves us, passionately, personally, deeply — and that love changes us, makes us into creatures who are strong and brave enough to care for others, strong and brave enough to trust in a power and strength beyond ourselves. It gives us power and strength displayed in the vulnerability of Christ on the cross. It gives power and strength that allows us to put down our petty worries and pick up the cross of Christ. It is this power and strength that sets us free from ourselves and binds us to the perfect freedom of service to Christ.

Amen.

Proper 20 / Ordinary Time 25 / Pentecost 17

Proverbs 31:10-31; Psalm 1; Mark 9:30-37

Repetition, Repetition, Repetition

They were on the road, going up to Jerusalem, and Jesus was walking ahead of them; they were amazed, and those who followed were afraid. He took the twelve aside again and began to tell them what was to happen to him, saying, *See, we are going up to Jerusalem, and the Son of Man will be handed over to the chief priests and the scribes, and they will condemn him to death; then they will hand him over to the Gentiles; they will mock him, and spit upon him, and flog him, and kill him; and after three days he will rise again* Mark 10:32-34 (NRSV).

In two chapters of Mark's gospel, Jesus told his disciples in plain, concrete language that he was going to be tortured, killed, and would rise after three days. He did not speak metaphorically or with hidden meaning or intention. He told the inner circle, his session (Yes, I assume that Jesus was Presbyterian, but please substitute for own denomination's name for your congregational ruling board.) what lay ahead of him. The first time, Peter rebuked him. Six days later Jesus told them again, but they did not understand and were afraid to ask. The third time he told them, it doesn't say how they reacted. But the very next thing that happened was a dispute between James and John, two of the disciples on the executive committee who were brothers, who requested to sit on either side of Jesus in glory. This indicates to me that they still didn't get what Jesus was talking about. Jesus told them, repeated the message again, and repeated it a third time. Each time he told those closest to him and each time they didn't understand.

I take a great interest in helping and mentoring people who are new to the ministry. The way I see it, I learned so much from my mistakes that it's a shame to waste them, so I try to teach others from my experiences.

One bit of advice I give to new ministers is, "Listen to the stories that people tell. When people repeat their stories, repeat your listening. Try to find out why this story is so important."

I used to visit a member of my church who would tell me what he did during World War II. He worked as an electrical engineer, designing equipment for planes. He had several patents to his credit and was quite proud of the work he had done in the war effort. But he also told me how hard he had tried to enlist in the army. One day he enlisted and the next day he was sent back to work. The next week he tried to enlist in a different city but was prevented from doing so. The government and his employer conspired to keep him out of uniform and keep him at his drafting table. It was quite a story, — and when I heard it the third time I realized that he felt guilty, embarrassed, maybe even ashamed — 40 plus years after the war ended, that he had served his country from the safety of his office, rather than in the trenches of war.

It wasn't so much what the man said, but that he said it several times that I began to look deeper to see what was really important.

There aren't many things that Jesus told his disciples three times in one gospel. He certainly did not repeat himself three times in three chapters about anything else but his coming death and resurrection. He told them openly, plainly, to put it in modern terms he was completely transparent and still they just… didn't… get… it….

I was at a preaching conference two decades ago and at the start of the first meeting we were asked, "What's your greatest fear as a preacher?"

Someone shouted, "Repeating myself!"

"Okay. What's your second greatest fear as preacher?"

A voice from the other side of the room shouted, "Repeating myself!"

Preachers live in fear of repeating ourselves. I keep a log on my desk and I record in it stories and illustrations I use to make a particular point, lest I repeat one. When I'm teaching Bible classes, I watch people's faces carefully, because I often forget which session I have given the speech about digging biblical manuscripts out of the ground, scribal errors, or Hebrew vowel points. I love to give these speeches, I treasure, even seek, to make these digressions, but do not want to repeat myself - especially when there is so little time for the class in the first place.

Jesus repeated himself as he spoke to his disciples. He gave the same message to them three times in the course of about two weeks. He spoke bluntly and they didn't understand. Jesus didn't fear repeating himself because his message was so important.

I know that repetition is an important part of education. My two-year-old is learning to count these days. I count the steps for him as we go down and he repeats. Now he knows there's a number past two. He won't learn his numbers if we only count one time. He needs to hear them and repeat them.

At our last church supper, we were talking about Matthew's version of the Lord's Prayer; it's different from Luke's. There were about a dozen people there and none of us remembered when we learned the Lord's prayer. We must have learned it in Sunday school, or at home, or maybe even from reciting it every week during worship. It was the repetition that etched the words permanently into our memories.

Jesus told his disciples three times that he was going to be tortured and killed. He told them he would rise again after three days. He told them. Six days later he told them again. He told them a third time, just before going into Jerusalem, on the eve of what we call Palm Sunday. He kept telling them.

Each time, the very next thing that happened in scripture was a discussion of personal status. Maybe a better term would be something like "our personal response" to Jesus' news of death and resurrection. First, Jesus said that to follow him one must deny oneself and take up one's cross. Next, in the gospel lesson for this morning, the disciples had been arguing about which of them was the greatest — but Jesus pointed out that the last shall be first, and welcoming a child is the same as welcoming God.

Jesus' call to service and sacrifice in this week's gospel lesson, just like last week's lesson, doesn't have any immediate, obvious appeal. To be great we are instructed to be servants. To be exalted and praised we are instructed to reach out to the people who are the least able to repay us for our efforts. We are to offer hospitality — that is, we are to say, and mean — that strangers are welcome, that it is well that they have come to visit, that we are pleased that they have to come to visit — to people who do not have homes to which they can welcome us in return. Jesus told his disciples that there was no *quid pro quo* offered to those who follow him.

And yet… and yet…

I assure you that there is compensation to taking up one's cross and following Christ. And there is compensation for those who agree to serve as deacons and elders in this congregation. Let me very clear about this right now — the compensation I speak of is not monetary. No one will make any money by being a deacon. But there is reward.

Our deacons visit the members of the congregation who cannot attend worship. Many of these people have been members for decades. The joy they feel in having contact with this church, in hearing what's going on here, in knowing that the work of the church continues is contagious.

Two years ago, I did a funeral for one of our long-standing members. This man's grandson told me he believed in God, but he also believed he could do good (yes, "good" is a noun here.) without taking part in the life of a church. He gave donations to food pantries and homeless shelters when he felt like it. It made him feel good. Maybe it even made him feel virtuous. What he didn't see was that his grandfather's church, especially the deacons, had looked after his grandfather faithfully. They did this, not because there was anything in it for them, but because that's what we do. Every one of the deacons who visited this man felt a friendship with him that was its own reward. In offering kindness, attention, or time to those who cannot pay us back we witness to the gospel faithfully.

This month we have started looking for deacons and elders to serve on our boards. While the deacons oversee ministries of caring, elders who serve on the session make virtually every decision that we make as a congregation.

There is power one could say, in service as an elder, but I've never known anyone at this church agree to serve because they were seeking power. Many agree to serve because they know their gifts are needed by the church. Others agree to serve because they believe passionately that the church needs to move in new directions. I try to emphasize that leadership in the church is servant leadership, after the model of Christ's sacrifice. I think it's irresponsible to say that taking a term on the board of deacons or the session will be easy or that the commitment is negligible. Serving has costs, it takes time and energy; it requires us to use our minds, our hearts, and our hands.

And yet... and yet... responding to the Holy Spirit's call to serve also has rewards. You may discover that you have interests and abilities you didn't realize. You will make new friends and deepen existing friendships. You will learn — I insist on that! — and you will be given opportunities to respond to Christ's call, to Christ's sacrifice. Something he told us about openly and plainly. In working for the church, using the energy, intelligence, imagination and love that God has given you, you will find joy and compensation. When the call comes — remember the call comes from God, through the voice of the congregation — please give the congregation's request of the spirit to use for the common good, give the request some serious, prayerful consideration.

Amen.

Esther 7:1-6, 9-10; 9:20-22; Psalm 124; Mark 9:38-50;
Numbers 11:4-6, 10-16, 24-29

It's Lonely At The Top

Our Old Testament lessons this morning show us two leaders who were terrified. Esther, Queen of the Babylonians, wife of King Ahasuerus, had just thrown a second feast for the king and his right-hand man, Haman. She had invited the two men to a feast the night before, but could not find the courage to ask the king to spare her people.

It's a long story. Esther was a Jew who was living in exile in Babylon. Her Uncle Mordecai was a prominent official in the palace. Haman, however, was a more powerful official in the palace. Haman insisted that people bowed before him, as before the king. Mordecai would not do that; as a pious Jew, bowing before anything other than God almighty would be idolatrous. Mordecai's defiance earned Haman's wrath. Haman convinced the king to send a message throughout the empire that all the Jews should be killed on a certain day. (The specific date was determined by throwing dice. The name of the Jewish festival that honors Esther's bravery is called "Purim," which is Hebrew for "dice.")

Esther had replaced Vashti as queen. King Ahasuerus, during one of his lavish parties wanted to show all the guests how beautiful Vashti was by having her appear before the guests wearing only her crown; Vashti refused to let that happen. Such defiance, the king was informed, could spread throughout the kingdom. His advisors suggested the king remove Vashti from the throne and find another queen. Something like a beauty contest was conducted and Esther won!

When Mordecai told Esther about Haman's plan of genocide, Esther did not know what to do. If she approached the king without being summoned, she could be killed. Esther was afraid. Mordecai suggested that perhaps Esther had become queen for such a time as this. Perhaps her beauty and status would win her the king's ear and she could get him to call for the slaughter of her people to end, as Esther did not want the Jews to be killed.

Esther thought about it and invited Haman and King Ahasuerus for the first feast. She did not make her request at the first banquet. Instead, she made another request... that the two men come to a second banquet, the one covered in today's reading, when Esther found her voice and revealed that it was Haman who planned the annihilation of her people. The king was enraged. One of the men in attendance to the king pointed out that there was already a gallows that had been built. Haman had built it for Mordecai's execution. How convenient. Haman was hung from the gallows he had built for the defiant Mordecai. The plan was called off. Esther's courage, and Mordecai's pleading, saved the Jewish people.

This morning's psalm could have been written as a celebratory anthem to be sung at the end of the book of Esther. *The Lord has come to our rescue!* It's good to pair this psalm with the Esther story. Esther is one of only two books in the whole Bible that do not mention God. (The other is Song of Songs.) Still, the faithful can sense the Lord's working through ordinary, flawed, human people to achieve great things. Actually, if God wanted to work with people, the best God can get is flawed, human, broken people. It's been said that Jesus was a friend of sinners, but what choice did he have, really?

In the lesson from Numbers we find another leader who knew it could be lonely at the top. The Hebrews were whining to Moses. They were tired of manna. They recalled all the delicious food they enjoyed in Egypt. Through the eyes of nostalgia, slavery looked pretty good. At least they got three squares a day, and there was a little variety in the menu. Moses was sick and tired of leading the people. It was too big a job! Moses didn't ask for this gig! He was not the Hebrews' mother and father. If God really wanted to do something nice for Moses, he'd simply kill him right then and there.

This latest tirade got the Lord's attention. The Lord created something like a session for Moses. Seventy trusted leaders received some of the Spirit that Moses had. And there were those two new leaders, El-dad and Me-dad, who did not get the memo. They did not go the tent to get the Spirit; they stayed in the camp. What should Moses do about that? I imagine a weary Moses muttering, "What? They stayed here and got it? Fine. Good for them, now let me get some rest."

In the gospel lesson a similar thing happened. John, a member of Jesus' inner circle' was upset because he had seen someone casting out demons in Jesus' name. Apparently, this individual had not paid the franchise fee. Jesus was undisturbed. He had bigger things to worry about than people driving out demons in his name. (Imagine what Moses would say! Find me another ten like that one and I can retire early!)

The last line of today's gospel reading was a little puzzling. Jesus talked about how good salt was. It's a preservative; it can be used as money; it seasons food, (There's a Danish proverb that one needs only two things to make good food: salt and an appetite.) but what good is salt if it loses its saltiness? Jesus concluded with this enigmatic phrase, "Have salt in yourselves, and be at peace with one another." Mark 9:50 (NRSV).

What could Jesus have meant by this? We've heard people described as "the salt of the earth," but what does that mean? When someone is "worth their salt" that means they're worth what they are paid. The word "salary" is rooted in "salt." What does it mean to have salt in oneself? Salt is valuable. It tastes good. It preserves food. We know now that sodium and chlorine are essential for the brain to function properly. But to have salt in yourself?

Maybe this is the notion that ties the readings together. Being a leader takes courage, vision, and energy. It's hard work. It's demanding work. But even in the midst of serious, existential threats, none of these leaders were really alone. Esther had Mordecai. Moses had the Lord, then a sizable board of directors. Jesus had his disciples — and it appears, some freelancers. None of these leaders was ever truly alone. The burden on leadership is heavy and taxing, but much easier to bear when one is not leading in isolation.

Yes, it's lonely at the top, but it doesn't have to be! Have salt in yourself, and in those around you. Good leadership is rooted in deep integrity — the salt in oneself Jesus spoke of, but good leaders must also have good "followership." If it's lonely at the top, realize that it doesn't have to be.

When geese migrate, the hardest — working goose is the one at the point of the V. That goose (both geese and ganders take this position) encounters the most resistance and has to work the hardest. The point position is rotated frequently. But the ones who are not up front have work to do too. They are back there, enjoying an easier flight and honking encouragement up to the front. If you think it's lonely at the top, then rotate back and let another leader take the point. And be sure to honk encouragement all the time.

Amen.

Proper 22 / Ordinary Time 27 / Pentecost 19

Psalm 8; Hebrews 1:1-4, 2:5-12; Mark 10:2-16

What's In A Name?

What do you think when you hear the name "Jesus?" What thoughts, images, metaphors come to your mind when you hear that name? We know a lot about Jesus' life; we have stories about what happened before he was born, when he was born, one in Luke's gospel about Jesus at age twelve, when he was a man, starting with his baptism and ending with how he died. We even have four stories about what happened after his death. Scripture gives us a lot of information and a lot of details about his life. The hymns we sing, (some of you have been singing them for more than ninety years!) give us ways to imagine Jesus..."Gentle Jesus;" "Savior;" "Like a shepherd;" "Beneath the Cross of Jesus;" "Ah, Holy Jesus;" "When Jesus Wept;" "Jesus Loves Me!" "Blessed Assurance, Jesus is Mine;" "What a Friend We Have in Jesus;" ...I could go on and on, just from our hymnal. Each of these hymns could trigger memories for some of you and give you mental pictures of Jesus.

I'm convinced though, that in our own life, in our personal prayer times, in moments of private devotion, when we raise spontaneous prayers, most of us are pretty lazy - or at least uncreative in how we address God and how we picture Jesus. Think about the words we use to begin prayers. I know someone who begins by saying, "Dear God..." which is good. It makes her prayers feel like letters to God, or it makes them sound like personal conversations with someone who is very close. (Whom do you call "dear?") But those two words can quickly become a formula and lose their meaning. I'm convinced that we need to think more broadly about God, in fact, we need to think about God in Christ as broadly as we possibly can.

Augustine said, "If you can imagine it, then it's not God." (St.

Augustine Quotes, *St. Augustine R.C. Church*, staugny.org/quotes) Knowing that words will always fall short of describing the reality of God should spur us to be more creative and more imaginative. I try to begin prayers spoken in worship in a variety of ways. Sometimes I get stuck on "master of the universe" which is a name for God favored by many Jews. Sometimes "mighty" or "holy" God works. When Jesus taught his disciples the prayer we call the Lord's Prayer he began in a startling way, he said, "Abba," which really means something like "Daddy."

The words we use shape the way we think. In fact, the words we use *define* the way we think about things and *define* ways we cannot think about things. If you doubt that words have power, remember God created the whole universe in six days and the only thing God did was speak.

This morning's lesson from Hebrews challenges us to see who Jesus is in ways that we are not accustomed to. I counted twelve different images or metaphors for Jesus in the twelve verses we read from Hebrews. That's too many for us to hold in our minds at one time as we ponder Christ and pray in Christ's name. But it's good for us to encounter images that are difficult or foreign to us because it will help us grow in faith.

Image #1 "Son." Hebrews 1:2 (NRSV). — We know that Jesus is God's son, born of the Virgin Mary, that Jesus is God's only begotten son. Our oldest creed tells us that. We know God's son was born to a fairly poor family in a small town, not in a family of wealth or power.

Image #2 "Heir." Hebrews 1:2 (NRSV). — God's son was the heir; that is, the one who would inherit the Father's estate. The one who had been entrusted to look after the Father's interests. The one who was trusted and chosen to continue what the Father had begun. The word "heir" has the same root as "inherit" and "heredity."

Image #3 — "The one through whom God created the world." Hebrews 1:2 (NRSV). Long-standing Christian theology says that all three persons in the Trinity have always existed. Rather than God the Father making Jesus, as described in the genealogy at the start of Matthew's gospel, and God making the Holy Spirit, as we might conclude from reading the second chapter of Acts, all three Father, Son, and Holy Spirit have always existed and have always been together. Here, Hebrews tells us that Jesus was present with God at creation.

Images #4 and #5 "The reflection of God's glory" and "the exact imprint of God's very being." Hebrews 1:3 (NRSV). These are two strong images which, though different, lead us to the same conclusion. Jesus is God. God and Jesus are the same. There isn't a shade of difference between the identities of Jesus and God.

Image #6 "Sustainer." Hebrews 1:3 (NRSV). — It says "[Jesus] Hebrews 1:3 (NRSV) sustains all things by his powerful words." This is more in keeping with the role we usually assign to the Holy Spirit. But remember, Christians believe that Christ, God, and the Holy Spirit have always existed, so it's appropriate, even orthodox, to say that Jesus sustains all things. One of the ways people talk about the Trinity in modern times is as Creator, redeemer, and sustainer, in place of the more familiar Father, Son, and Holy Ghost/Spirit. In this text we understand that Jesus also is our sustainer.

Image #7 — "Purifier for sins." Hebrews 1:3 (NRSV). There is a distinction between being clean and being pure. We're clean when we wash our hands. Clean means we're free from dirt, but to be pure requires a ritual cleansing, a special kind of washing. Ritual purity is more than just being clean, it is the removal of what keeps a person from participating fully in the life of a community. Jesus, this image tells us, removes all the impurity that keeps us from being with other believers — and keeps us from fellowship with God. Our sin, our impurity, is a barrier that keeps us isolated from other people and from God. But Jesus makes a way for us. Our sin, though serious, is less powerful than the power of Jesus's sacrifice, which atones for our sin and makes us whole again.

Image #8 — "Much superior to angels." Hebrews 1:4 (NRSV). Angels are very popular now, people have always talked about guardian angels. Recently I heard about an organization that was planning "Angel Con," similar to "Comic Con," the nirvana for comic book geeks' annual event. People who go to Angel Con would be surrounded by other people who are experts in angelology and passionate about angels. In this image we have Jesus described as superior to angels. That implies some kind of hierarchy — as if God is at the top, then angels, then people, then animals and plants. The author of Hebrews cites this morning's psalm that describes angels squarely in the middle between God and humanity. This image puts Jesus up there with God, above the angels and well above humanity.

A word about angels. Angels are messengers. Every place they appear in scripture they bring news, sometimes tidings of good news of great joy for all people. Sometimes not. In Luke's gospel, the first thing the angel says to the shepherds when it announced Jesus' birth is "Do not be afraid." Then that angel was joined by an army of angels. That's what "heavenly host" means, an army of angels.

The word "evangelism" has "angel" right in the middle, because evangelists carry good news. I hope that we are all both angels and evangelists.

Image #9 — "For a little while, lower than the angels." Hebrews 2:7 (NRSV). When Jesus was on earth and lived as a man, Jesus was down on the level of humanity, but now he's up above again. This image is of central importance to Christians because it tells us that God understands what we feel and think. God understands the pain of abandonment and the horrible physical pain of crucifixion because God in Christ felt it. God's not remote and untouched by our longings, pain, and suffering. (The lyrics from "Christ is Alive!," an Easter hymn, states "Not throned afar, remotely high/ Untouched, unmoved by human pains/But daily, in the midst of life/Our Savior, in the God-head reigns.") God has been there with us. God has been there as one of us, and it is my firm belief that what God endured as Christ on the cross changed God, making God see humanity as both more precious and more vulnerable than before.

Image #10 — Jesus was "crowned with glory and honor." Hebrews 2:7 (NRSV). These are words we mostly hear in church. Once in a while someone received an "honor" or is "honored" with an award, but "glory" is just about the sole domain of the church. Both have to do with importance and respect. For Jesus to be crowned with honor and glory is to be the most respected, most important being in heaven. Certainly that is the case because it goes on to say that Jesus, because of the suffering of death on the cross, has risen to the highest position.

Image #11 — "The pioneer of salvation." Hebrews 2:10 (NRSV). This is is the one that really jumped out at me when I first looked at this text. I love the image of Jesus as an American pioneer, riding across the Great Plains in a Conestoga wagon, wearing a flannel shirt. I mean, that's what pioneers did, wasn't it? Yes, in our national history that's what pioneers did, but in general, pioneers are the ones who go first and find a way for others to follow. Pioneers are the ones who blaze the trails for those who come after them. Louis Pasteur was a pioneer because he realized that things too small to see made people sick. Jackie Robinson was a pioneer. Alan Shepherd and Chuck Yeager were pioneers. They went first; it's dangerous to go first. The first ones are the ones who are misunderstood. The first ones don't have anyone to ask for directions. They're the ones who are brave beyond courage. And they are strong from within. Think of how that applies to Jesus. He blazed a trail for us. He went first by rising from the grave. He has gone before us to prepare a place for us. He's the one who makes us safe — eternally safe and secure.

We're almost done, Image #12 — the last way the text helps us imagine Jesus is as "the one who sanctifies." Hebrews 2:11 (NRSV). Sanctify is another church word, no one ever uses that word anywhere else. Jesus, our sanctifier, removes sin from us, and makes us holy. That's what it means to be sanctified — we are set apart as holy, set apart for God's use and we're free of sin.

Twelve images are a lot. Too many to absorb and put to use at once. But as I say after a big meal, "the message of the gospel is abundance." There should be more than we can hope to comprehend - more than we can hope to use. There should be too many images for us to see anything clearly. Hold onto one and you'll miss the others. Son… heir… Creator… reflection of God's glory… exact imprint of God's very being… sustainer… purifier… superior to angels… below angels for a time… crowned with honor and glory… pioneer of salvation… sanctifier….

Hold onto as many of them as help you understand how good God is to us, in sending part of Godself to turn us around, wash us and make us new. Celebrate God's love for you. It is a love that is beyond our ability to understand.

Amen.

Proper 23 / Ordinary Time 28 / Pentecost 20

Psalm 90:12-17; Hebrews 4:12-16; Mark 10:17-31

Recush רכוש

The title for today's sermon is an obscure Hebrew word. I remember it more than 25 years after first learning it because my professor made it memorable. We were studying the passage in Genesis where Abraham heard that his nephew Lot had been taken hostage. Abraham went to battle to free Lot and "brought back all the goods (*recush*, רכוש) and also brought back his nephew Lot." Genesis 14:16 (NRSV). "Goods" is a really vague word. It's like our word "stuff." We asked what "goods" would entail and our professor said, "Tupperware.®" In other passages it is translated "utensils" or "moveable property." *Recush* is stuff that is portable.

We have *an abundance* of recush at my house. I expect you have a lot of *recush* at your house. The ironic thing to me is that all this "moveable property" makes it hard for us to move. And I mean "move" in both senses—relocate, as in move to a different address, and move—as in get from one room to another.

I am preaching to myself today as much as anyone else. I grew up in a family that was shaped by The Great Depression. I expect many of you did too. Some of you grew up during The Depression. In my family, thrift was a virtue, a strength of character, which was valued as highly as honesty. We hated to see anything go to waste. My wife's family had a similar mindset. Her mother had a sampler hanging in her kitchen that read: "Use it up. Wear it out. Make it do. Do without."

I know I am not alone in having a lot of *recush*. We moved into our house twenty years ago. In the rafters in the garage there was a cupboard that contained a dozen perfectly good, empty Hills Bros.™ coffee cans. I laughed when I found them. I'm certain the former owner had forgotten about them, or maybe he remembered and the one way to get away from them was to sell the house! Did I say they're perfectly good? Those two words make it very difficult for me — and I'm pretty sure for many of you also — to get rid of them. Full disclosure — I didn't get rid of them. I took them to church; the Sunday school covered them with paper and glitter and a few times a year we pull them out for a "joyful noise" offering. People are encouraged to throw coins into them and it's fun and silly, plus the money supports programs for kids… and I get a frisson of joy, knowing those coffee cans have been put to good use! We used them last week when we covered the story of Esther. Some of you had cans that you could rattle every time you heard the name "Haman," the villain of the story.

Here's the part of the story that becomes confessional for me: When I pulled out one of those cans last Sunday, I found it contained fifteen film canisters. Every single one of them was perfectly good. I could not throw them away. They're great to keep in the car, in case you need change for a toll or a parking meter. Who wants one, or two - or fifteen? They're free to a good home. I can't simply throw them out… they're perfectly good! Oh, and they're plastic, so they're good for the next 10,000 years or so. "Tom," you may be thinking, "you could recycle them!" Well, not exactly, the caps are made of a kind of plastic that is not currently recycled in this county.

A man came to Jesus and asked a simple question: "What must I do to inherit eternal life?" It's a simple question, but also a confusing question. One cannot do anything to get an inheritance. It is up to the one who owns the property to decide who will inherit it. The man wanted to know how to get his ticket to heaven punched. While it does not say this, it is pretty clear that the man was well off. He was educated and later it said that, "he had many possessions" Mark 10:22 (NRSV). He had been a faithful adherent to all the religious laws. Just ask him! But then Jesus said something that is a bit of a paradox. "You lack one thing." Probably the man did not lack any *thing.* So what did he lack? Could you describe what he lacked in a word or two?

We talked about this at Bible study recently. The consensus was that it was not the fact the man had lots of possessions, but that he was so attached to his possessions. He was attached to his wealth. It was as though his stuff owned him. These words really got my attention: "He was shocked and went away grieving, for he had many possessions." He was shocked. He had been obedient all his life. He knew the law and kept it. He was secure. He was safe.

Jesus called him to a radical trust. I look around my office. I look around my house. I am surrounded by stuff. Would I be grieved if I gave all my possessions away? What would that be like?

[At this point I am reminded of a cartoon that was in the New Yorker a few years ago. There is an enormous plastic bag in a field with a twist tie on it. A man with a beatific smile is walking away. The caption was something like "The life-altering moment of walking away from everything you own."]

I imagine refugees right now, leaving Eritrea, Syria, Iraq, and Central America. They are walking and carrying their most precious possessions. You can't carry very much. What would it be like to walk away from your home? You are carrying and wearing — you hope — what you will need to get to a safe place and start a new life, in a nation where you do not speak the language or even understand how to shop for food. They're driven to desperation, and if they can prove "a well-founded fear of persecution," they may be granted refugee status. They are leaving home because they fear for their lives.

What did the man who knelt before Jesus in today's lesson fear? I think he was afraid of letting go of what made him feel secure: his stuff. It was easier for him to trust his stuff — or perhaps it was harder for him to give his stuff up than to trust Jesus. It's a hard lesson. And it's especially hard for us who have grown up with lives shaped by the fear of scarcity. It's especially hard for those of us who equate frugality with responsibility and virtue to trust that there will be enough. It's fear, but it's even more subtle than fear — it's the fear of regret of giving something away that we might want in the future. We're afraid we might part with something and regret not having it at some point in the future.

As I was sitting in my office writing those last two paragraphs, I walked to my book shelves and found more than twenty books that I would never miss. Some I read years ago. Many were assigned in seminary. Some I took from the libraries of colleagues who were retiring and wanted me to take them. I took this stack of books to the public library and donated them for their next book sale. I still have books that I will never open, let alone read. It was easy to part with these books because I didn't even know I had them, so I cannot miss them.

We live in a place where we have enough of everything. We actually have more than enough of most things. Jesus calls us to trust and follow. One thing Jesus never commanded his followers to do was hoard, protect, and guard our possessions. Jesus called us to trust him and follow. That's scary. And it's even more scary for people like us who have so much.

I've preached on *recush* before and some people were motivated and went home and cleaned out a closet! They gave some of their *recush* to Goodwill or Saint Vinny's. That's a start, I suppose, and I'm always gratified whenever someone tells me they've paid attention to one of my sermons - but I hope you'll stay with the shock and sadness of the man who came to Jesus. It really looks to me that his possessions were blocking him from a life of dynamic faith.

I expect each of us owns more than he did. Do your possessions bring you joy? I asked myself that question as I walked home for lunch last week. I spotted a sugar maple tree that was alive with bright red leaves, and it was a sunny day, so the red leaves contrasted with the blue sky. That tree brought me joy. That tree reminded me of God's love and the goodness of creation. That tree even made me happier than dropping off a load of books at the library.

Amen.

Proper 24 / Ordinary Time 29 / Pentecost 21

Psalm 104:1-9, 24, 35c; Mark 10:35-45

Baptized In Water

For the past month in our gospel readings, Jesus has been making his way to Jerusalem. He has been preparing his disciples for what awaited him there. They have rebuked him, been afraid to ask what he meant, and squabbled over who would have positions of leadership in his movement after he left them. Mixed in with his instruction and preparation to his disciples are stories of Jesus healing people seized with demons, disputing with the Pharisees, and lifting up the needs of children and "little ones," those weak in their belief and new to the Christian faith. While this is happening they were slowly working their way to Jerusalem. The clock was ticking and the disciples *still* didn't get it.

This morning it's James and John, two of the inner circle, the executive committee of the twelve, the two who, with Peter, went up the mountain with Jesus and saw him transfigured into a dazzling brightness while he talked with Elijah and Moses. They asked a favor of Jesus; they wanted positions of power, status, and authority with Jesus in glory.

Jesus made an interesting response; he asked, "Are you able to drink the cup that I drink or be baptized with the baptism that I am baptized with?" Mark 10:38 (NRSV). He was making reference to some images from the Old Testament that are not widely remembered. The cup that Jesus spoke of was the cup of wrath, which symbolized God's judgment of human or national sin. To drink from the cup of wrath was to be punished. When Israel returned from exile in Babylon, God spoke to the prophets Isaiah and Jeremiah, saying that they had drunk all they needed to from the cup of wrath. Elsewhere in scripture, cups were used to symbolize one's fate. In Old Testament times people understood that there was only so much of anything. If they were blessed with an abundance of food; that meant someone else was going hungry. In the same way, if one was afflicted with trouble, say drinking from the cup of calamity, then someone else wasn't. They viewed the world as a zero sum game, which meant that the cup of wrath didn't go away, but another nation had to drink from it.

In Matthew's gospel when Jesus was praying in Gethsemane he prayed, "let this cup pass from me." Matthew 26:39 (NRSV). About a week earlier he'd asked James and John if they were able to drink from the same cup, they said that they were, but that night in the garden, they could not stay awake. They said they could drink from the cup that Jesus would drink from but they couldn't. They abandoned him just as Peter and the other disciples had.

Jesus also asked if they could be baptized with his baptism. Before Christians like (*here insert the name of the person most recently baptized in your congregation)* were baptized in the name of the Father, the Son and the Holy Spirit, Jews regarded passing through water as a sign of trial. Psalm 69 begins:

> *Save me, O God,for the waters have come up to my neck. I sink in deep mire,where there is no foothold....*
>
> Psalm 69:1-2 (NRSV)

And in the 43rd chapter of Isaiah, the Lord reassured the prophet:

> *When you pass through the waters, I will be with you,*
> *And through the rivers, they shall not overwhelm you....*
>
> Isaiah 43:2 (NRSV)

Passing through water had great significance for a people who had fled slavery, pursued by a mighty army, which was drowned in the sea. Passing though water had great significance for a nation that finally reached the promised land after each tribe set a stone in the Jordan River and the waters piled up so they could cross the riverbed on dry ground. Even today we talk about being "swamped" or "drowning" when the amount of work overwhelms us. This was the baptism that Jesus spoke of to James and John on the way to Jerusalem. It was a much graver kind of baptism, a much deeper kind of baptism than the one Jesus had at the Jordan River. That was a baptism of repentance, a sign of turning away from one old way of life. That was a sign of turning over a new leaf and making a fresh start.

Jews had been practicing baptism of repentance for generations before John the Baptizer baptized Jesus. (A quick note about that terminology: many people in today's society hear "Baptism" the same way as "Presbyterian," that is, identified with a specific denomination. When John was baptizing out at the Jordan River, when he wasn't eating bugs and honey, he was a "baptizer;" there were no "Baptists" back then.)

Perhaps you're wondering which type of baptism we do here, which kind we have whenever a family presents a child to be baptized, or when an older person asks to be baptized. Is it the kind that Jesus talked about in response to James and John, in which one is overwhelmed by the chaotic power of a flood? Or is it a baptism that marks a turning point in one's life, a washing, a cleansing? In our tradition it is both — we hold up water's power to destroy and its power to cleanse. We hold up the fact that water is essential for life on earth but also can be perilous and destructive. "Baptism points us back to the grace of God expressed in Jesus Christ, who died for us and who was raised for us. Baptism points us forward to that same Christ who will fulfill God's purpose in God's promised future." (*The Book of Order* (Louisville, KY: Office of the General Presbyterian Assembly, W-2.3002.)

All this talk about cups and baptisms is important because some of the disciples were looking ahead to a future where they expected to be rewarded. Even though they repeatedly misunderstood what Jesus told them plainly, they still were looking ahead to power and status. Christ surprised them - again. Before, he had told them they had to take up their cross and follow him and that they had to become like little children. But in this morning's lesson from Mark, he told them plainly that they were not like the Gentile leaders who lorded over their people as tyrants. He said: If you want to be great, be a servant, and if you want to be first, you must be a slave of all. It was not the path they wanted to take. But it's the path Christ invites us all to take.

And it's the path that Jesus himself took - to serve - to die - to set us free.

It's a path of sacrifice, a path of cups of wrath and flood waters. It is not easy glory or cheap grace. It's a path of shared burdens and joy at the knowledge of God's presence in our midst. It is the joy we celebrate every time we celebrate the sacrament. A joy that the universal church of Jesus Christ shared whenever someone is baptized. Remember, we are baptized into Christ's death… and resurrection.

With that baptism we also make a commitment. Churches promise to take on the duty, the responsibility of sharing the good news of life in Christ with the newly baptized one. No one is a Christian alone. The joy we share binds us together, as does our call to serve binds us together. Just as our gratitude to Christ for dying for our sins binds us together. Just as our call to serve God in Christ on this side of the cross binds us together, with a mission, and a purpose and an identity, in this joy we are in Christ.

Amen.

Proper 25 / Ordinary Time 30 / Pentecost 22

Psalm 34:1-8, (19-22); Jeremiah 31:7-9; Psalm 126; Mark 10:46-52

Seeing With The Eyes Of Faith

We've been walking with Jesus on the way to Jerusalem for over a month. The stories from Mark's gospel have showed us many sides of Jesus' personality. Perhaps more importantly, they have shown us many sides of the disciples' personalities. The disciples in many ways took our place in that drama. They reacted as we would, most of the time, I think. They were slow to understand that Jesus was going to suffer and die. They were more concerned about their own status and power than anything else. They overlooked children and people who were new to the faith. They didn't want to hear it when Jesus said he was going to die. These stories have all come from about a three chapter long "hinge" in Mark's gospel. It was the literal turning point, when Jesus turned toward Jerusalem and began heading there. During this hinge in the gospel a remarkable thing happened: Jesus changed. Jesus was different when the transition was completed than he was before it.

Remember that Jesus is one of the three persons of the Trinity. Jesus is God. So to say Jesus changed is to say that God changed. Let me be clear about that, because I know that in Sunday school and confirmation and other places, many of us were taught that God is unchanging. But I don't believe that. Scripture showed us God who is a creator and sustaining presence and a savior. Scripture used many images for God because we need many images to describe God who is beyond description. I'll use just one example: God the Father. We know what fathers do — they love their children, protect their children, provide for their children, teach and discipline their children, praise their children, set limits for their children, comfort, encourage, admonish… and the list goes on and on and on. A good father doesn't always encourage, he isn't an *unchanging* encourager. An ideal father knows exactly what his child needs and that changes from minute to minute. Ideal fathers, I contend, always love and protect their children, in that way they are unchanging, but precisely how love and protection are extended happens in a myriad of ways. So it is with God, who, we believe, loves us constantly. Loving us when we face surgery is different from loving us when we are sound asleep, driving to work, or getting a haircut. God's love is constant, but God is flexible in expressing that love to us. So God loves us in different ways from one moment to the next. The best image for God's loving us constantly, in different ways, is the sky. The sky is always changing. It's always there, and I need to be able to see the sky all the time. I can't stand being in rooms without windows. Still, I rarely look at the ever-changing sky. We take the sky for granted, we don't notice it unless something really big or dramatic like a beautiful sunset or an ominous cloud seizes our attention. Like the sky, God's love is always there, and always changing.

Back to Jesus' change. In the eighth chapter of Mark's gospel, when Jesus was way up north in Bethsaida, along the Sea of Galilee, some people brought a blind man to him. Jesus took the man by the hand, led him away from the village, put saliva on the man's eyes and then the man said he saw trees walking around. "Then Jesus laid hands on him again; and he looked intently and his sight was restored" Mark 8:25 (NRSV). Then Jesus sent the man home and said, "Do not even go into the village." Jesus performed this miracle in private; it was difficult — he had to touch the man twice — we don't know this man's name; and Jesus' instruction had the effect of keeping the healing secret. Compare that to the lesson for today.

Jesus was in Jericho, much closer to Jerusalem, only two days' journey away. We know this blind man's name, Bartimaeus, and we even know his father's name. The crowd didn't bring him forward, the crowd tried to keep him back. Jesus didn't touch Bartimeaus, he only said that his faith had made him well Mark 10: 46-52 (NRSV). All that took place in the middle of the crowd, with many witnesses looking on, the disciples, and others who were forming up into a parade. We see

Jesus at a different point in his ministry. It had become public and he was facing Jerusalem. He had warned his disciples for what lied ahead; at least he tried to warn them. He was more decisive, and more powerful in this story than earlier in Mark's gospel.

Immediately ("immediately" was Mark's favorite word!) Bartimeaus followed Jesus. I think that was the point of the story. That once someone has put his faith in Christ, blindness suddenly turns to sight. People see clearly. Bartimaeus saw so clearly that he followed Jesus right as he was heading into Jerusalem, heading up to the temple on the day we call Palm Sunday. This turning point in the blind man's life was the end of the turning point for Jesus. From this moment on, the events unfolded with a purpose, as though the gospel was a movie in which all the elements of the plot had come together for the conclusion.

But look at the crowd. Look at the ones who told the blind man to be still, not to bother the savior. "Many sternly ordered him to be quiet, but he cried out even more loudly" Mark 10:48 (NRSV). Who was blind in this story? Who couldn't see what was in plain view? Certainly it was the crowd, those who had gathered around Jesus, those who were about to parade with him up to the temple. Who saw clearly? Certainly it was the one who couldn't see at all! It was the one who would not be silenced — even though it was inconvenient and irritating to the people in the crowd.

Whom do we overlook? Who among us sees things clearly, but is one we want to silence? Who has the courage to stand up in a crowd and call out for what they need? This blind man, the persistent one, the one who would not be kept out, he was the one who got to write a poem like this morning's lesson from Psalm 34:

I sought the Lord and he answered me,
And delivered me from all my fears
Look to him, and be radiant;
So your faces shall never be ashamed.

Psalm 34:4-5 (NRSV)

Psalm 34 also contains one of my favorite verses: "O taste and see that the Lord is good." Any time you want to take a second dessert at a church potluck, say that verse; enjoying dessert should be a chance to deepen your faith!

This poor soul cried, and was heard by the Lord and was saved from every trouble. You see, it's the one who cries out, the one who seeks the Lord's help, who gets it. It is not the ones who are self-contained and self-satisfied. It's the persistent who are heard and healed. And it's the persistent who are grateful and who are changed.

Did you notice the joy, the celebration in the lesson from Jeremiah? Of all the prophets, Jeremiah was the one who most honestly spoke of how he had suffered for answering God's call. He was a laughing stock, he was mocked and humiliated, and he accused God of deceiving (other translations say "seducing") him. But Jeremiah had remained true and spoken God's word, even when it was unpopular and unwanted. After the leaders and royalty were carried off to Babylon and only a few people remained behind in the ruins of Jerusalem, God had Jeremiah speak a word of restoration. The Lord said that he had become a father. Jeremiah's faith throughout his suffering was changed and transformed.

The persistent blind man turned to follow Jesus because he had changed.

A few months ago someone gave me a perfect description of my prayer life. I can practically summarize my prayers into two categories: "Help me, help me, help me" and "thank you, thank you, thank you." Certainly the prayers I raise spontaneously in the course of my workday fall into one of those categories. But when my "help me" prayers are answered, and my "thank you" prayers are over — see, the two are linked, they're the same prayer, really — I am rarely changed as profoundly as Bartimaeus was. I go back to being what I was before I needed and I called out for God's help. I blend back in with the crowd - a crowd that would really rather not have dealt with a noisy blind guy who needed Jesus' attention. Maybe Bartimaeus did the same thing. There is no other mention of him in the Bible. Maybe once he got his sight back he blended in with the crowd that was following Jesus. Maybe he added his voice to those who didn't want Jesus to turn aside and pay attention to a blind beggar. But I don't think that's what happened. I think Bartimaeus had one of those life-changing encounters with the Son of God and was changed forever. A lot of people come to know Christ as Lord and Savior that way. They can suddenly see; their faith makes them whole again. And they turn to follow.

Most of us, at least most of the people who talk about their faith around here, say that they need to keep turning back. We stray. We sin. We forget. We need to turn around — every day — every hour. We need to keep turning away from selfishness. We need to keep turning away from the crowd — whoever the crowd may be. And we need to keep turning, returning, to follow after Christ. We know what Bartimaeus did when he could see, but we never heard whether it was easy for him to stay faithful to Jesus.

Most of us are in the crowd. The crowd that tries to keep the blind beggar silent. We need to recognize that we have a role in this story and we're not the stars or the heroes. What makes scripture powerful is that it forces us to recognize that we're not always that noble; we're not always the good guys; we're not always right.

Last week I was talking to a couple of ministers about the hardest theological questions. We are all in denominations that have ministers examine candidates for ministry prior to ordination. I said that one question I always struggle with — and thus one question I always ask candidates for ministry — is about the atonement. What does it mean, how do you understand it, that Jesus Christ died for your sins? One of my colleagues gave me a new way to understand it, a new metaphor for this difficult theological concept. He said the atonement was an accident. There was a baby crawling across a road and an out-of-control truck was barreling down a hill. The truck couldn't stop in time to keep from running over the baby. Suddenly someone ran into the middle of the road, threw the baby out of the truck's path and was killed instantly. Jesus was the man who saved the baby. Who are we? We're the baby. Who are we? We're the one driving the truck.

In our lesson from Mark this morning, who are you? The man who was filled with joy at being able to see? The one who turned to follow Jesus? Are you part of the crowd, urging the persistent blind man to keep quiet? It's both, isn't it? Jesus calls to both parts of you — the faithful eager follower and the stubborn. He calls to the blind crowd member — he calls and calls. And he invites. His call is persistent and faithful. He's calling us even now.

Amen.

Proper 26 / Ordinary Time 31 / Pentecost 23

Ruth 1:1-18; Psalm 146; Deuteronomy 6:1-9; Psalm 119:1-8; Hebrews 9:11-14; Mark 12:28-34

Bread For The Journey

I spent a lot of my adolescence on church mission trips. We called them work camps back then. Every time the church van was about to leave the parking lot, just after the driver had turned the ignition key someone would ask, "How long 'til we get there?"

Now, when I'm behind the wheel I give the same answer, that was given to me' "Over a few hills, around a few bends, we're practically there." I can repeat this answer more times than the asker repeats the question. I can be very patient. Back in the day, my evasive, non-answer would have sent the more curious travelers to the road maps in the glove compartment. I learned, "Over a few hills, around a few bends, we're practically there," from the pastor who led the trips I went on in high school. For him, it wasn't evasion; it was the truth as he saw it! I'll never forget the time I was riding shotgun, navigating as we headed for Sioux City, Iowa. We had written directions, but I couldn't find the exit from the I-road that we were supposed to take. There was a simple reason for this, our destination was not Sioux City, Iowa, but Sioux Falls, South Dakota. My pastor had underestimated the number of hills and bends. The miscalculation meant that we had to drive about 90 miles farther than expected. It was really more though. Everyone knows that the Midwest expands in July and August. It felt more like another 200 miles!

Journeys are like that, even well-planned journeys have their share of unexpected twists in the road. That's what makes travelling interesting and risky. Jesus told the scribe that his journey was nearly at an end, when he said, "You are not far from the kingdom of God."

Mark 12:34 (NRSV). That's the phrase I tripped over this week. What did Jesus mean? Was this a compliment, a challenge, or an invitation?

Jesus engaged in many conversations with the religious authorities of his time. His message was often offensive to them. Earlier in this very important chapter of Mark's gospel, Jesus told the parable about the wicked tenants and when those hearing the story "realized that he had told the parable against them, they wanted to arrest him," but they didn't because they were afraid of the crowd Mark 12:12 (NRSV).

When they asked Jesus whether they should pay taxes and he looked at a coin and said, "Give to the emperor the things that are the emperor's and give to God the things that are God's" — they were utterly amazed at him Mark 12:17 (NRSV).

When the Sadducees tried to trap him by cleverly asking him about the resurrection, his response left them speechless.

Then along came the scribe from today's passage. This is the only story in the whole New Testament in which a religious figure sincerely approached Jesus with a question. The scribe was not trying to trick Jesus or trap him in a battle of words and wits. He was genuinely curious and wanted to know what Jesus believed was the most important commandment. Jesus' answer was what Christians today call "the summary of the law." It's a combination of verses from Deuteronomy and Leviticus that emphasized that love was — and is — the most important thing of all, love for the Lord and love for one's neighbors. That is the essence of how God calls us to live. This passage is like an ancient story of a man who approached the great Rabbi Hillel and asked the scholar to teach him the entire Torah while he stood on one foot. The rabbi's famous response was, "What is hateful to you, do not do to your neighbor: that is the whole Torah, the rest is commentary." (Rabbi Hillel, "Babylonian Talmud," Shabbath folio 31a. http://www.judentum.org/talmud/trakate/shabbath/shabbath_31.html).

In our passage, the scribe agreed with Jesus and even went on to say that love was more important than sacrificial offerings. Jesus said, "You are not far from the kingdom of God." It was as if Jesus was saying, "You're on the right track, but there are a few more bends to go around and hills to go over, before you've really arrived." The story left us hanging in mid-journey. We don't know whether the man completed his journey and "arrived" or if he stayed "not far" from the kingdom of God.

Today is Reformation Sunday, the day when churches who trace their heritage to Martin Luther, John Calvin, and few other reformers remember and celebrate the roads that we have travelled through history. This is a day when we can look back to the thoughts and ideas that have guided us for over 500 years. One of the central concepts behind the Reformation is that the church should continually be reforming itself. As long as the Holy Spirit is at work in the world, the church must be prepared to follow where it leads. The church must always be ready to respond to the pain of the world and scripture is there to guide us as we try to discern God's will in the present. The work of the church is to always be in the process of getting nearer to the kingdom of God. We are always dependent on God's grace, so we know that no matter how hard we work to further our journey, any progress we make is a gift from God.

There was a message on the back of the big tour buses that my marching band used to use when I was in college that read, "Getting there is half the fun." We never believed it. For us *getting there* meant riding a bus for eight hours to places like Bloomington, Indiana, and East Lansing, Michigan. (It also meant getting clobbered by superior football teams — in the rain. The futility of rooting for Northwestern in the 1980s was terrific preparation for parish ministry.) For us, the bus ride was a necessary evil, a means to getting where we really wanted to go. Getting there was not half the fun at all; it was boring. Being there — wherever *there* might be — was all the fun. We didn't enjoy the journey, in our hearts we were always asking, 'How long until we get there?"

"Getting there is half the fun" is a good slogan for Presbyterians, because we take great care whenever we make a decision. We insist on hearing as many points of view as possible. As a denomination, we do not jump to quick, simple answers. Instead we believe that the

Holy Spirit works through congregations, task forces, committees, and ruling councils. We believe that decisions we reach together — guided by the Holy Spirit — bring honor and glory to God. For Presbyterians the process that we go through in making decisions is practically as important as the decision itself.

Once at a Presbytery meeting when we faced a vote on an issue on which we were deeply divided, the moderator declared that we would vote by paper ballot. Someone protested, so we had a vote on whether to use paper ballots or to vote by voice. The debate was intense. The Presbytery voted to use paper ballots by a narrow margin. The vote on the controversial topic itself was much more lopsided. The most interesting vote of the day was a vote on how to vote! Do you see why Presbyterians sometimes seem baffling and odd to other Christians?

This is why we need to love the process and to love the journey. It helps if we really believe that "getting there is half the fun," because the road is often so long and has so many bends and hills that it seems that we'll never arrive anywhere.

The reading from Ruth this morning is the very beginning of Ruth's journey to a foreign land, the land of her in-laws. After her father-in-law, husband, and brother-in-law died, her mother-in-law, Naomi, decided to return to her hometown, Bethlehem. Naomi intended to go alone, but Ruth insisted on going back home with her. Naomi was grieving the death of her husband and sons, but allowed Ruth to come along anyway. In the second chapter of the book, Ruth went out to glean in a field near Bethlehem. Gleaning was a kind of food share program during that time. Harvesters did not pick every bit of produce and did not pick up anything that fell to the ground. They left those bits for needy people who followed the harvesters. Ruth just happened to glean in a field of a relative of her husband. She was a hard worker. She gained the attention of the field's owner, Boaz. Naomi schemed and got Ruth to seek protection from Boaz. In her case, protection was a man who could marry her. Ruth was a foreign widow, which made her very vulnerable to being exploited, some translations say, 'molested.' The very end of the story is a moment of triumph for Naomi, who was thrilled at the birth of her grandson. Oh, and her grandson was the father of Jesse who was the father of David, a former ruddy shepherd boy, composer of psalms and a great king — that guy.

Ruth was quite literally the first convert to Judaism. Her journey from her home - the beginning of which we covered in today's reading — a foreign place out of loyalty to her mother-in-law had a truly happy ending. One can see the guidance of the Holy Spirit prior to Ruth's journey and well beyond it.

We find a very faithful, trusting journeyer in this morning's lesson from First Kings. Elijah was in hot water, which was incongruous in that he had just prophesied a drought. In so doing, he challenged Baal, the god that King Ahab and his wife, Jezebel, had been worshiping, against the Lord who had brought the Israelites out of Egypt with a mighty hand and an outstretched arm. (That's a travel story for another time.) Elijah fled into the wilderness at God's command. He had enough water there and ravens brought him food. As today's lesson started, Elijah's water source had dried up, so God had instructed him to journey to Sidon, where a widow would care for him. He found the widow, who was herself close to starving, along with her son. Elijah told her to bring him a small cake made from the tiny amount of flour and oil that she had on hand. He declared that the oil and meal would not run out until the rain returned. She cared for Elijah for many days. When the widow's son was close to death, Elijah was able to bring him back to life through prayer. Elijah was a good man to have around the house. We just get a glimpse of his journey this morning. I doubt that he would say "Getting there is half the fun." Like all Old Testament prophets, Elijah paid a high price for speaking the words of the Lord.

Every work camp I have led has had many highpoints and memories. You can never tell when a certain vignette or encounter will be a story that gets told back home that in some way captures and summarizes the entire trip. We always tell those stories when we return.

There are, however, two high points on every mission trip that can be scheduled with precision. For me personally, the first one comes behind the wheel of the church van about thirty minutes after pulling out of the church parking lot. We've stopped waving, we haven't gotten into the snacks that we packed - our bread for the journey. We're just far enough away from home that if something goes wrong, the group is going to have to improvise. All the careful planning — believe me, every vehicle has detailed directions to every destination, I never want to head to the wrong state again! - cannot prevent difficulties from emerging. I have found that it is those difficulties, the ones that arise after we're too far away to turn around, are what memories are made of. Once a father wished me a trouble-free trip and I replied, "There would be nothing to remember! Give me a trip with troubles that we can work through, with difficulties that we overcome together, by working as a team." That moment when we leave the church parking lot's gravitation field always gives me a frisson of excitement.

The other moment comes either on the last night or the last lunch stop on our way back home. We gather around the Lord's table, which may be a picnic table just off the I-road, and we share the Lord's Supper. This is the sacrament that Christ commanded his followers to do to remember him. This is the sacrament that reminds us that we are one in Christ. At the end of a work camp when we're tired and eager to get home, it's good to pause for a moment and remember what we have been through, together, on the journey that we are about to complete.

As Christians we're all on a journey, even if that journey doesn't lead us to another city. What's your journey like?

How has your journey of faith been surprising?

What obstacles do you face on your journey, what roadblocks?

How have you felt the leadership of Christ on your journey?

How have you been aware of the presence of the Holy Spirit on your journey?

What do you need to strengthen and encourage you as you look at the next step you will take?

We are all in this together. Let us resolve to be open to whatever is at work in us and among us and finally, enjoy the journey which Christ invites all of us to take.

Amen.

All Saints' Day

John 11:32-44; Isaiah 25:6-9; Revelation 21:1-6a; Psalm 24

The Rhythm Of The Saints

Sometimes Protestants find it difficult to know how to observe All Saints' Day. I have lived in several communities that have a very strong Roman Catholic presence. Protestants do not venerate or pray to saints, but we can and should claim the idea of saints as an important part of our faith. The term appears a few times in the psalms but is most conspicuously present in Paul's correspondence to the first Christian churches. Paul, it seemed, was always sending greetings to the saints in other communities, asking to be remembered to the saints in the communities where he had made friends and started churches. Here's the part of All Saints' Day that Protestants can claim: the word appears in the Bible, so we ought to take it seriously. Every place it appears in the Bible, it is plural. (The only exception is when Paul conveys greetings to "greet every saint in Christ Jesus" Philippians 4:21 (NRSV).

Protestants do not recognize individual saints. For us, saints are always a community — always. Other names for saints could be "believers" or "church members." Everyone who is in Christ is a saint; we're *all* saints. We just do not use the term often. If someone was to ask me how many saints there are in the church I serve, I would probably think it was a trick question. But if I was to answer honestly, with biblical accuracy, I would say, "all of them."

Look at the other people who are here in worship this morning. They are all made in God's image; *we* are all made in God's image. We are altogether, a community of saints.

Last month, when we celebrated World Communion Sunday, we recognized that Christians are literally in every country on earth. As a Presbyterian, I laugh at our thoroughness: when World Communion

Sunday was first observed, one thing the organizers made sure of was that the Lord's Supper would be celebrated in every time zone on earth. Only a Presbyterian would think of that. That celebration reminds us that we are part of a global fellowship, a catholic, (small "c") that is, universal church.

All Saints' Day reminds us that we are also linked to other Christians/saints through time. In the book of Hebrews we find that marvelous phrase, "so great a cloud of witnesses" Hebrews 12:1 (NRSV) who have gone before us. Christians are not born; we are made. People who have learned the faith before we were born have handed it on to us, and our sacred duty is to pass the *good news of new life* in Jesus Christ to people who will come after us. All Saints' Day reminds us that we are also linked through the ages, through time, not just across great distances but also language and cultural barriers.

I called these remarks "the rhythm of the saints" because of the musician Paul Simon. Over thirty years ago, Paul Simon released an album (I'm showing my age, I know) called "The Rhythm of the Saints." He had gone to South America and encountered different styles of music and different instruments that he had never known of before. He brought together musicians from many countries and recorded with them in Argentina. One of the indigenous communities he encountered did a lot of drumming. Each member of the community had his or her own distinct rhythm. Try to think of their rhythm as their signature. The people would all get together and make music, each contributing something unique to the music that they made altogether. I think this is a wonderful image for every Christian congregation. On a day when we look back and remember saints who were part of this community, before joining the great cloud of witnesses, think of how each one brought something to the "music" we all make together as we strive to be the *church* of Jesus Christ, the *body* of Christ in this particular time and place. The music we make together now is different, it has been diminished by the loss of certain rhythms.

All Saints' Day can only be bitter and sweet. Consider the friendship Jesus had with Mary, Martha, and Lazarus. Rather than looking at the miracle of bringing Lazarus back to life after four days, I want you to notice how the community acted when Jesus arrived. Mary was weeping, and she had other mourners with her, all weeping. Jesus was deeply moved, and very empathic. Then Jesus himself wept. If you ever doubt that Jesus was fully human, point yourself to this verse. Jesus cried with other people who were crying because someone they loved had died. They were all in this together. That's what saints do.

I remember a story of a group of preschoolers who visited a group of seniors in a nursing home. One little girl sat with an elderly man in his wheelchair. The man was lonely and also sad because his wife of more than five decades had died the week before. When the teacher asked the girl what the little girl did, she responded, "I helped him cry." *Everyone* has a rhythm to contribute to the music the saints make together!

Our psalm this morning reminds us that all of creation is the Lord's and it has all been filled to overflowing by God's abundance and generosity. The psalm should prompt us to pause, to slow down at least a little, and look around at the blessings that surround us each and every day. We can lift our heads high, when we remember God's profound love for all of us, and when we remember that God's love for the saints does not end at death. The strongest passage in scripture, in my opinion is in Paul's letter to the Christians in Rome in which he said "Nor anything else in all creation has any power to separate us from the love of God in Christ Jesus our Lord." Romans 8:39 (NRSV). Paul wrote that after listing things that threatened the Roman Christians. One of the things that threatened them — and all of us — is death, but even death cannot separate us from the relentless love God sends to us through Christ.

I have to close with the passage from Revelation. It's a description, even though every description we could even imagine will fall short of the amazing moment described when the Lord dwells fully with humanity and humanity with the Lord. The great cloud of witnesses has been joined by all those loved and claimed by the eternal God. Death and suffering will be no more. Our lesson from Isaiah makes a similar point, "death will be swallowed up." 1 Corinthians 15:54 (NRSV). That makes me think, as much as I loved reading the Harry Potter books with my sons — and I'll admit it, rereading them myself — I was always puzzled that the forces of evil were called "death eaters." Isn't eating death precisely what both Isaiah and Revelation described? "Death will be no more." "He will swallow up death forever." Those don't just sound like good news, they sound like *the best possible news of all time!!*

What we celebrate on All Saints' Day can be described in a prayer I use toward the end of funerals and memorial services, "…we thank you, for her death is passed and pain is ended, and she has entered the joy that you have prepared…." Of course we're sad as we remember people whom we loved, who helped us grow in faith, but we're also happy that they are now dwelling completely, wholly, in the joy prepared for them. That joy that awaits us, when even the great cloud of witnesses will be outshone by the eternal light of the living God.

Amen.

Proper 27 / Ordinary Time 32 / Pentecost 24

Ruth 3:1-5, 4:13-17; Psalm 146; Mark 12:38-44

Good News From The Threshing Floor

Harvest time is a good time to tell the story of Ruth. Ruth is one of two books in the Bible named after women, the other is Esther. One could argue that the book could be more accurately named for Ruth's mother-in-law, Naomi. Our lesson for this morning gives the denouement, the happy ending, of Ruth's saga. To get a true picture of how her story applies to us today we need to cover some of the background, some of what happened before Ruth went to the threshing room in her best dress.

In what Christians call the Old Testament, the book of Ruth follows the book of Judges. That's the logical place for it. The book of Ruth begins, "In the days when the judges ruled..." Ruth 1:1 (NRSV). It is worth noting, however, that the Hebrew scriptures have a different sequence. In that version, the book of Ruth follows Proverbs. The last part of Proverbs is an ode to the *Eshet Ḥayil*. There is not a precise translation for this term. It can be rendered as "women of valor" or "capable wife." The book of Ruth follows this poem in praise of the ideal woman. It is as though Ruth was the personification of all the attributes listed in the twenty verses that conclude the book of Proverbs.

Back to the story of Ruth. Ruth and another woman named Orpah married two sons of Elimelech and Naomi. The story began in Moab, but Elimelech's family was from Bethlehem. All three men died and Naomi decided to return to her home. Orpah and Ruth decided to go with her. Naomi advised them not to. Orpah heeded Naomi's advice, but Ruth was determined to stay with Naomi. Some translations have Ruth saying something like, "Entreat me not to leave you." Ruth 1:16 (NKJV). Those words are the name of a song that used to be commonly performed at weddings. There is a delightful irony of a song based on a daughter-in-law's devotion to her mother-in-law being sung at weddings! A more faithful rendering of what Ruth said captures the young widow's determination. Something like, "Don't press me to leave you.... Your people... my people... your God, my God... your resting place, my resting place...." Ruth 1:16-17 (NRSV). Ruth's passion was so strong Naomi stopped arguing.

Bethlehem was buzzing like a beehive when Naomi returned, but Naomi was a changed woman. She was a widow with her widowed daughter-in-law in tow and she told the community to call her "Mara" then. "Mara" means "bitter." "Naomi" means something like "sweet" or "pleasant." The Lord "has brought calamity on me," Naomi said. Ruth 1:21 (NRSV). Ruth and Naomi returned to Bethlehem at the time of the barley harvest.

In the second chapter Ruth, the young foreign widow, went to work gleaning in a local field. This was a kind of welfare program in biblical times. After a field had been harvested, people were permitted to go through the field and pick up any grain that the harvesters left. The Torah instructed owners of fields to not harvest to the very edges of their fields.

Ruth got to work gleaning and her diligence was noticed by Boaz, a prominent man, the owner of the field. Boaz instructed his harvesting crew not to molest Ruth and to leave some choice bits of grain for her. At lunch time, he gave Ruth a large portion of food. She couldn't finish it all, so she took some back to Naomi. Ruth's diligent gleaning had been bountiful. When she brought her haul home to Naomi, Ruth learned that the field where she worked belonged to a relative of Naomi. This gets us up to today's reading from Ruth.

As the reading begins, Naomi instructed Ruth to anoint herself and to put on her best clothes... she was not going to Bethlehem's formal ball, but she was going to the place where Boaz was going to thresh his barley! Naomi told her to wait until the barley was threshed and Boaz had had enough to drink that he fell into a contented sleep. Then, Naomi instructed Ruth to uncover Boaz's feet while he was asleep. "Feet" is a Hebrew scriptures euphemism for "naughty bits," which is itself a euphemism. You know what I mean.

When Boaz was startled into wakefulness, he was probably feeling a little chilly, he was surprised that Ruth was there, asking him to spread his cloak over her. Ruth informed him that he was her next of kin. Ruth was seeking a kind of physical and societal protection from Boaz. He could cover her with his clothes, but there was another man who was a closer relative than he. Ruth didn't know about that. Then, before anyone else was awake, Boaz loaded Ruth down with more grain. They both behaved honorably in the barley pile.

There was a little drama at the start of the fourth chapter of Ruth. Boaz went to the gate of the city and talked to the man who was a closer relative. The other man would have purchased the field if Ruth was not part of the deal. He chose not to buy the field and acquire Ruth as his wife. Boaz was scrupulous in following the legal customs of purchasing a field.

This scene is a lot like what Jesus said of the scribes in this morning's gospel lesson. The scribes loved to walk around in their Guccis and tailor-made suits. They sat in the skybox at the synagogue, they orated lengthy eloquent prayers, but they preyed on widows like Ruth!

And speaking of widows, toward the end of this morning's psalm reading we are reminded that, "The Lord watches over the strangers; he upholds the orphan and the widow..." Psalm 146:9 (NRSV). Ruth was both a widow and a stranger.

The happy (and significant) ending of the book of Ruth is the last part of today's passage. Note that it was Naomi who nursed the child. It was the women who were buzzing like a beehive (The Hebrew *bah om* is the word that described Bethlehem when Naomi returned. It is an onomatopoeia for the sound a beehive makes.) who named the child. Ruth was completely absent from the story after her son, Obed, was born.

Here's why all this matters: Ruth was the first convert to Judaism. She was a Moabite who won acceptance, favor, and a family through her diligence and virtue. She was good to her mother-in-law; she was honorable with the man who covered and protected her. She followed

Naomi's instructions. She became the mother of Obed, the grandmother of Jesse and the great-grandmother of David. Remember David's hometown? It was Bethlehem.

Ruth was one of three women before Mary named in the genealogy of Jesus at the start of the gospel of Matthew. She was a foreigner, a convert. Another woman mentioned in the genealogy was Rahab, the prostitute in Jericho who hid the two Israelite spies who had gone on a scouting mission into the Promised Land. The first of the three women mentioned was Tamar. Tamar's right to Levirate marriage to one of Judah's sons was thwarted by Judah, who decided she was cursed after his sons Er and Onan died, leaving her childless. Tamar acted as a prostitute and conceived twins with Judah. It's a long story, best told at another time.

Ruth was among three woman, all of them outsiders or in other ways notorious, who were part of our Lord and Savior's bloodline. Look what the Lord can do, even working through flawed, human people like us!

Amen.

Proper 28 / Ordinary Time 33 / Pentecost 25

1 Samuel 1:4-20; 1 Samuel 2:1-10; Hebrews 10:11-14, (15-18), 19-25; Mark 13:1-8

Steadfast Change

When I first looked at the texts for today, I immediately thought of the difference between change and transformation. I realized that I'm probably looking too closely at words again, looking more deeply at them than anyone cares about. But in the context of this congregation, it seems to me that change is inevitable and transformation is coming. I've felt it for a while.

People fear change and even resist it, but the fact is that as long as we are alive, we are changing. That means that when we proclaim that Christ is alive, we are claiming that Christ is changing and even that Christ is the agent of change. And yet, scripture also says that Christ is the same yesterday, today, and forever, so which is it? It seems to me that Christ is unchanging because the grace God offers us through Christ is always available to us and is always precisely what we need to be whole, complete, and accepted by God. The love we know in Christ Jesus is constant. But the shape of that love, the ways it is revealed to us, the ways that we are able to recognize, articulate, and share that love with others is changing with the circumstances, contexts and situations we find ourselves in. As Christians we say, "God is love." As Presbyterians we say, "God is free." Free to exceed the limits we impose on God, free to love us relentlessly, and even to love relentlessly those whom we have deemed unlovable, free to shape us and shape history however God chooses. When God called Moses out of the fire of the burning bush, Moses asked what to call God, by knowing God's name he'd have some power over God. The name God gave himself was "I am who I am." Exodus 3:14 (NRSV). There is an ancient Jewish tradition that renders that name, "I will be everything tomorrow demands." Even

God's name tells us that God is free — and the freedom is one that exceeds what we can conceive about God.

Change is inevitable in all things that are living. Today, for example, you are the oldest you have ever been, and you'll never be this young again. Our church community is different, diminished because of the people who have recently died or moved away. Even if we tried to seal the way things are in this congregation and fight change with everything we've got, we will change. We are changing whether we accept or deny that fact.

Transformation is also inevitable, but transformation is a more radical altering than mere change. Transformation is a change that, in my opinion, requires divine assistance. We can seek to change ourselves, but to be transformed we have to let God work through us. In fact, after thinking about these two words for a few weeks I looked them up. One synonym for "transform" is "convert." I should point out at this point that one definition of change is "absence of monotony." That definition took me by surprise and I think it should take churches like ours by surprise, because the mainline Protestant churches have been in decline for more than a generation in this country. Not only is the national percentage of Lutherans, Methodists, Episcopalians, Presbyterians, and United Churches of Christ dropping — and although we certainly have less influence on the culture at large than we did fifty years ago, our absolute numbers of members are also dropping. In fact, every year of my life has seen a decrease in the number of Presbyterians in the United States. One reason for this is that our worship services are boring — for thirty years I've heard of us referred to as "God's frozen people." It seems to me that there is a third option — we are not forced to choose between changing and being transformed. We could choose to stay in the rut we have been in as individuals, as congregations, and denominations, and change would come as we dwindle rapidly into irrelevance or navel-gazing.

We could coast or cruise control or auto-pilot as some have accused us of over the years, but first, let's look at what God can do to bring new life.

"In those days there was no king in Israel, everyone did what was right in their own eyes." Judges 17:6 (NRSV). That's the description of Israelite society as the book of Judges described it. For some time the Israelites had clambered for a king; all the cool countries had kings, they wanted one too. At this point in the story we are introduced to Hannah, a woman with a lot of problems. In our Old Testament lesson today she is described as "deeply distressed," "severely provoked," "barren." She "wept bitterly," and was mistaken for a "drunken spectacle," although she explained that she was "deeply troubled," and in "great anxiety and vexation." She "poured out her soul in prayer."

I don't watch TV shows that bring people before live studio audiences to hear how awful their lives are, but I'm pretty sure Hannah would have been a good candidate for a show like that. She was the favored wife of Elkanah, but Elkanah's other wife, Peninnah, although she was not well-loved, had given Elkanah sons and daughters. Peninnah was mean to Hannah. For his part, Elkanah was a little dense. He asked Hannah, "Why do you weep?" and "Am I not more to you than ten sons?" 1 Samuel 1:8 (NRSV). Well, no, Elkanah, the fact was you were not worth more than ten sons to Hannah. She was in misery. Today we might say that she had "hit rock bottom." Hannah turned to God in prayer at Shiloh where she and Elkanah and Peninnah and all of Peninnah's children went once a year to offer sacrifices. The priest spotted Hannah while she was standing at the temple, weeping, moving her lips but not saying anything.

Eli, the priest, assumed that she was drunk. In a nice word play, Hannah said, "I'm not drunk, I'm pouring out my soul before the Lord." 1 Samuel 1:15 (NRSV). And Eli waved his hand and said, "Go in peace, the God of Israel grant the petition you made him." This breaks me up because Eli didn't know what Hannah was praying for! I can picture Eli wanting to lock up after a busy day saying, "Yeah, yeah, whatever." And yet, Hannah went away and she wasn't sad anymore. Maybe that's because Eli said she would have her petition granted, but it seems to me it was just as likely that it was because Eli actually recognized that Hannah was deeply distressed — he didn't find out what the problem was, but at least he understood that there was a problem. That's more than her husband, her husband's other wife, or any of the other wife's bratty kids did.

Hannah made a vow. She had a son and named him Samuel, which means, "I have asked him of the Lord." And then she lent the son that she had longed for to God. Samuel became sort of a priestly intern. Later, he replaced Eli himself as priest. And it was Samuel who anointed Israel's first king, Saul, and its second and greatest king, David. See, it wasn't only Hannah's life that was transformed, though her life certainly was transformed. After Samuel, Hannah had other children whom she did not lend to the Lord's service, children whom she did not vow to make Nazirites. The history of the world was changed by Hannah's prayer.

Our gospel lesson gives a radically different look at change. Jesus was preparing his disciples for what they would face after he died. False messiahs, people who claimed to be the Savior come back, wars and rumors of wars, earthquakes, famines… and we could think, well, obviously he was talking about current times. I wonder about the news coverage that was around in Jesus' day. I mean today we have round-the-clock news and the internet. When there's an earth tremor in Japan, we know about it. And we know about what our nation's drones are doing in distant lands. Famines in Ethiopia and sub-Saharan Africa are so frequent that folks in the first world have developed "compassion fatigue." I doubt that wars and famines are more common today than in Jesus' time, but we certainly hear about them more readily.

Jesus said, "These are the birth pangs," to which his disciples must have asked, "Well, Jesus, when is the baby coming?" And we're still waiting. We are *still* waiting. Some of us have forgotten that. Most of us, probably. But the fact is we are waiting for the biggest change or transformation ever. We are waiting for Christ's return. And no one knows exactly when that will happen. In fact, Jesus said, "About the day and hour no one knows, neither the angels in heaven nor the son, but only the Father." This gives us an interesting loophole, I think. If no one knows the hour of Christ's return, then the one moment we can be certain that Christ will not return is when someone claims he will! We live on this side of history, and God is alive and present in this moment, but God is also above and outside of history, working in ways that we cannot begin to conceive.

The lesson from Hebrews this morning gives us another look at transformation. It shows us the radical change that Christ's death on the cross brought to the world. This passage offers a stark contrast to the way things had been before Christ — when priests offered sacrifices every day. The author of Hebrews pointed out that the very fact that they had to stand day after day offering the same sacrifices to please God showed that this simply didn't — and could never — work. We believe that Christ offered a single sacrifice for all time that took away our sin. That's why we have a table to gather around to remember Christ's death on the cross and not an altar where sacrifices are presented again and again. That's why we have pastors, shepherds that is, who lead and protect their flocks, not priests who conduct sacrifices.

Christ's death on the cross for our sin is the greatest possible change — the most radical transformation ever. In, fact, I would say that Christ's death on the cross changed God. On the cross, God felt the physical pain and the horror of abandonment and the power of God's love for humanity, for all of creation, was clearly revealed and more tenderly offered. God changed at the crucifixion.

That profound change is still effective. In fact, one sign of the completion of that change is that while the priests were described as standing, Christ was seated at God's right hand, not needing to rush into service.

Perhaps you're wondering what all this means — lessons of profound change from long ago, the observation that change is inevitable and transformation is possible. What does that mean for us? Just this: We need to open ourselves to how God is present with us and be ready to follow where God leads. Most of all I'm convinced we need to pray for this congregation, for the work that awaits us, for opportunities we do not yet recognize. Opportunities to be an example and a bearer of Christ's love in this community. We like to plan, control, and word our motions precisely, but we need to be ready, eager even, to look away from what's familiar and comfortable and find a risk worth taking for the gospel of Christ to be proclaimed here and now. We need to be attentive to something new, because the God we love and serve makes us, and all things, new.

Amen.

Reign of Christ / Ordinary Time 34 / Pentecost 26

2 Samuel 23:1-7; Psalm 132:1-12, (13-18); Daniel 7:9-10, 13-14; Psalm 93; Revelation 1:4b-8; John 18:33-37

Christ, Our King

Today is the last day of the church year. The church year starts four Sundays before Christmas, so next week when I wish you all a happy new year, I hope to get a better response than blank stares. The last Sunday of the church is called both "Christ the King" Sunday, and "Reign of Christ" Sunday. This festival goes all the way back to 1925, when Pope Pius XI added it to the calendar. It was set as the last Sunday of the church year in 1970. When I learned this I was a little surprised. I love looking into the history of our traditions and practices; I love learning about their origins and finding out why we do things the way we've always done them. But this is a new tradition. This is a holy day that has been set as the last Sunday of the church year during my lifetime!

The surprising things to me about the addition of Christ the King/ Reign of Christ Sunday to the calendar is that it came in an age when many, perhaps most, countries have elected, not dynastic governments. Perhaps this day was added to reacquaint Christians with being subjects. Looking at the long view of history, it's probable that most Christians through the ages have lived under kings, queens, and other kinds of non-elected rulers. But for us Americans who fought a revolution to drive out dynastic government, who built into our constitution the prohibition against bestowing titles — seriously, in the 1920s some people objected to calling Babe Ruth "the Sultan of Swat" and Benny Goodman "the King of Swing," a decade later — because *no royal titles*!

No Title of Nobility shall be granted by the United States: And no Person holding any Office of Profit or Trust under them, shall, without the Consent of the Congress, accept of any present, Emolument, Office, or Title, of any kind whatever, from any King, Prince, or foreign State.[US Constitution, Article VIII, Sec. IX, Clause XIII]

The office of king is, well, foreign to Americans. It is outside our experience in the way that shepherds are outside our experience. We read about shepherds all the time in the Bible, but have you ever met one?

Our experience with royalty is what we hear about the British royal family, but what does Queen Elizabeth *do?* She's surrounded by guards and traditions, and she lives in castles — oh, and she's surrounded by photographers; her children and her grandchildren are of immense interest, even to people in other nations. Anyone who's visited an American supermarket in the last forty years and looked at the magazines — admit it, you read the headlines! — would think the British royals rule us.

Seriously, what does the queen do? I'm asking two questions, neither of which I know the answer to: does Queen Elizabeth work? and also what is the nature of her power and authority? Can she create laws, can she veto legislation? Declare holidays? Declare war? I simply don't know. I do know this: her husband is not a king; he's a prince. A man does not become king in British tradition by marrying a queen, though women who marry kings become queens. It doesn't seem fair to me, somehow, but it's their tradition, their government, not mine.

What we know about kings is that they rule over particular pieces of ground, and have control over the people who live there. The saying, "A man's home is his castle," means that individuals rule over their homes in the same way that kings rule over nations. Kings have subjects. Nations have citizens, churches have members (although sometimes we slip and call them "giving units") but kings have subjects, and subjects are under the control of kings.

That brings me to the lessons from John's gospel, part of Jesus's trial before Pilate. Every time I come across this passage I remember

David Bowie playing Pilate in "*The Last Temptation of Christ*." Bowie's Pilate was icily indifferent as he cooed, "So, you are a king." *The Last Temptation of Christ*, directed by Martin Scorsese (1988; New York: Universal Pictures), DVD. He was aloof and disinterested in the film, but on closer reading I have to say I think the film got this scene wrong, it set the wrong tone. The contrast between Christ and Pilate was one of self-sufficiency and insecurity.

Pilate first appeared early in the morning of Jesus' arrest. The Jewish authorities brought Jesus to Pilate. (I need to clarify here that it was the Jewish authorities who were acting against Jesus. The gospel of John is often lazy in saying merely, "the Jews," as though all Jews everywhere are somehow responsible for the crucifixion. The seed of anti-Semitism can be replanted every time someone reads John's gospel and a few other New Testament texts without appreciating this distinction. John's gospel was certainly set in a context very different from ours, when John was being written Christianity was a sect within Judaism, [so the disputes like family feuds we find in John.]) Pilate asked, "What accusation do you bring against this man?" and the answer was, "If this man were not a criminal we wouldn't bring him to you." John 18: 29-30 (NRSV). There's nothing like not answering the question that has been asked — and that's *nothing* like answering the question that had been asked! Pilate correctly pointed out that there were Jewish courts in which to try people guilty of transgressing religious law. But those bringing Jesus pointed out that only Rome had the power to execute a criminal. Now think about this, Pilate didn't know what the charge against Jesus was, just that those bringing Jesus before him believed Jesus had committed a capital offense. Somehow, the text doesn't say how, Pilate learned that the charge against Jesus was that he claimed to be king.

It was in the exchange between Pilate and Jesus that the contrast between the two leaders, and their two kingdoms, became clear. Jesus was direct and transparent saying that his kingdom was not of this world. He said that his subjects were those who recognized truth. So his kingdom was not over a piece of land, rather it was over the hearts and minds of those who were brave enough to follow him. If his kingdom was like Pilate's, his followers would have been waging war — and many of Jesus' followers wanted to wage war, expecting the Messiah to lead that war — to drive the Roman occupiers out of their country. Many were disappointed that Jesus didn't start an uprising, that he wasn't a revolutionary, that the movement had prompted many people to follow him but wouldn't bring a change of government. This is the truth Jesus mentioned at the end of his conversation before Pilate, to which Pilate famously asked, "What is truth?" But then Pilate left Jesus and reported to the Jewish authorities, "I find no case against him." John 18:38 (NRSV). Apparently King Pilate was not threatened by King Jesus who claimed his kingdom was not of this world.

(A little Christmas foreshadowing here: Herod was *totally* afraid of a king, even a baby king, being born in his realm.)

Pilate offered to release Jesus, as was the custom of the Roman occupiers. One prisoner got released from custody every Passover. The Jewish authorities chose Barabbas, a failed revolutionary. Jesus was flogged, then Pilate again told the authorities that he found no case against Jesus. He presented Jesus to them a third time and said, "Crucify him yourselves, I find no case against him." John 19:6 (NRSV). But they pointed out that according to their law, anyone who claimed to be God's son must be killed. At this, finally, Pilate was afraid. He tried even more urgently to not have Jesus crucified, but the crowd yelled even louder. They pitted Pilate's fear of God against his ambition, saying, "If you release this man you are no friend of the emperor." John 19:12 (NRSV). The authorities did not seem troubled at all because the name Barabbas means, "son of the father" …hmm.

It's fascinating, this powerful ruler was fearful of one whose authority was not from this world. Pilate, in my opinion, got a glimpse of who Jesus was and what Jesus had come to do, but simply couldn't move much beyond his narrow, earthly understanding. And the more he tried to make others responsible for Christ's execution, the more eagerly the authorities proclaimed their allegiance to the emperor as well as to taking the responsibility on themselves.

To put this struggle in regal or authoritative terms, the more Pilate abdicated, the more the authorities sought to enthrone themselves as loyal subjects of the great and mighty emperor to whom their loyalty was unwavering.

What can this collision between two kings and two kingdoms mean to us today? Jesus said that no one can serve two masters — he was speaking of God and wealth at that point, but he could have been speaking about *many* of ways we divide our loyalty. Whom should we put on the throne? To whom should we give our loyalty? In the paper recently, I saw this ad for computer software and DVD programs about astronomy. I thought at first it was for telescopes — it caught my eye because of the words, "*Prove to your kids they're not the center of the universe.*" There was a man and a boy, presumably father and son, looking into the night sky with a telescope on a tripod.[1]

1 Image courtesy of Starry Night, www.StarryNight.com

I love astronomy. I love looking up into the night sky. Anytime there's an eclipse, aurora display, comet, super moon, or anything else unusual in the sky, I want to see it and want my family to see it with me. The psalms tell us the heavens declare the glory of God, and their vastness and beauty can teach us a proper humility. They can make us feel small, and in our feeling small we might even come face-to-face with a reality that we ignore in our day-to-day lives: We're not in charge. We believe we are powerful, autonomous beings, able to plan and control — if not world events at least our little corners of the world, our spheres of influence — our families, those with whom we work, our personal space — but looking up into the vastness of the heavens makes us stop and wonder. Pilate wasn't a guy who stopped and wondered much. But he did when he spoke to Jesus. In that conversation we saw how closely wonder and fear were linked. Stopping and wondering — whether prompted by gazing at the sky, marveling at God's love for humanity displayed on the cross or cherishing the embrace of someone we love — helps us to see that we are not the center of the universe, that we don't belong on the throne, but one more powerful and gentle than us does.

I'll never forget a moment when I got a glimpse of my place in the kingdom where Christ rules. I was standing under a starry sky, feeling that I had somehow been lifted into the air because the stars were all around me and I was so tiny. I looked straight up and suddenly realized that though I am a tiny, tiny part of the universe, there was nothing that separated me from God. I could look straight up into heaven and I did, for a long, long time. I didn't need to be king then, because I knew the difference between being an insignificant part of an infinite universe and being a tiny, treasure, beloved part of God's kingdom.

I admit it's a daily struggle to keep Christ on the throne in my heart; it's where he belongs and it's how I can best live as his loyal subject.

Amen.

Thanksgiving Day

Joel 2:21-27; Psalm 126; Matthew 6:25-33

Gratitude On The Prairie

Sylvan Grove, Kansas, is a community of about 200 people and 52 of them are members of the First Presbyterian Church. There is no Second Presbyterian Church in Sylvan Grove, Kansas. Like a lot of prairie communities, Sylvan Grove has been shrinking and aging. Young people who grew up there moved away. There are no employment prospects to draw young families. The biggest employer for miles around — also the most visible thing for miles around — is the grain elevator.

The good people of the First Presbyterian Church decided they wanted to do something for the community. They wanted to bring people together. There's another church in town, on the other side of town. It's a stricter brand of the same Christianity that the First Presbyterians observe. There isn't much interaction between the two churches. There's no ministerial association in Sylvan Grove, Kansas. Nothing brings the two churches together.

The idea the good people of the First Presbyterian Church came up with was to have a Christmas dinner in the church basement. They'd whip up turkey, potatoes, stuffing — you know what Christmas dinner is — and invite the whole community to eat their fill. No tickets, no calling ahead for reservations, no charge — just a gift because Christmas is the season of giving, you know.

Funny thing about Sylvan Grove, Kansas: even though the young people moved away, they still made their annual pilgrimages from Salina, Topeka, Wichita, even Denver, to visit their parents and grandparents back home at Christmas time.

Another funny thing about Christmas is that it can get kind of long, especially if you live alone. At first it was just older people, whose children had moved even farther away than Denver, too far to plan a trip to Sylvan Grove, Kansas, in late December… at first it was those people who found their way to the basement of the First Presbyterian Church and sat down on the metal folding chairs.

But even if you have family in, after the presents are opened and the wrappings taken care of, after the decorations have been admired, Christmas can get kind of long. It can even be a little stressful — all these beloved relatives together once a year can make a house feel small, a little crowded. A lot of these families decided that they'd just let the turkey stay in the freezer and mosey over to the Presbyterian Church. It was the only place in Lincoln County that was open for business, except for the Conoco station out on the I-road.

From the start, friends and neighbors drifted into the church basement. But later on families, three, even four generations together would troop down the stairs, hang up their coats, and make their way through the line.

And all these young people who had gone to school together saw their old buddies, classmates, and teammates. They met each other's husbands and wives. Their kids started bouncing off each other — just as they bounced off their cousins and siblings back at grandma and grandpa's. There was more room in the basement at First Presbyterian Church, so the noise didn't get to you so much.

Altogether the good people of the First Presbyterian Church of Sylvan Grove, Kansas, served 100 people that day. Nearly twice as many as the church members, enjoyed food, and hospitality that Christmas afternoon.

The people, the guests, wanted to give something back. They had such a good time sitting on the metal folding chairs in the church basement catching up, watching their children catch up, watching the children playing, eating a whole lot more food that they'd intended. They wanted to give something back. They wanted to say, "thank you" to the good people of First Presbyterian Church of Sylvan Grove, Kansas.

"No, no, no, this was our Christmas gift to you!" the servers and the cooks and the pastor said, over and over. "Please just let this be our gift to you!"

It was not to be. The guests had too good a time, they needed to pay for it, or to show their gratitude for it, or to help pay back for all the turkey and pie they had eaten.

There were no baskets on the tables for donations. Just some carnations that someone picked up two days before in Salina. No one stuck a sign next to the plates at the start of the line that said, "$2 is a good amount."

The guests got frustrated. Those who were so grateful didn't have a way to give back and the good people of the First Presbyterian Church of Sylvan Grove, Kansas, could not get their neighbors to understand that a gift was a gift. You say, "thank you," and that's the end of it!

A compromise was reached, sort of. I mean, there has to be a happy ending, right? The aprons that said "Have you hugged a Presbyterian today?" that the servers, cooks, and pastor wore had pockets in them. Someone got the bright idea of stuffing wadded up bills into the pockets of the aprons. You could sneak up behind someone and drop a little present in, or you could give someone a hug in Christian fellowship and, if you're quick enough about it you could make a drop into the pocket.

When everyone had headed home and the last drumstick and piece of pumpkin pie had been claimed, reluctantly, "Well, it's not like Marge and I need more pie, but a guy hates to see it go to waste," Vern said with a gleam in his eye, when the good people of the First Presbyterian Church of Sylvan Grove, Kansas, took off their aprons, they found more than $350 had been stuffed into the pockets!

I bet you've all had the experience of not being understood, right? You say something kind and helpful and people think you're being critical. You offer to hold a door for someone who you think might appreciate some help, but they want to do it themselves, not accept your offer to help. That's how the good people of the Presbyterian Church felt on Christmas afternoon when they discovered their windfall.

There's never a shortage of ways to spend money around the church, the Lincoln County Food Pantry was the beneficiary of the gratitude that had been expressed in wadded up dollar bills that found their way into the apron pockets.

It took the members of the First Presbyterian Church in Sylvan Grove, Kansas, a while to realize what they had done. It seems that simple hospitality isn't so simple anymore. Seems that roasting a turkey and sharing it with your neighbors is a rare thing these days. They just wanted to give people a place to go, but instead they held a *feast.* Usually feasts are planned, you know when they're coming; this one took everyone by surprise.

There in the basement of the First Presbyterian Church of Sylvan Grove, Kansas, the words of this morning's psalm were lived out and fulfilled.

When the Lord restored the fortunes of Zion,
(When you could smell the turkey up in the narthex)
we were like those who dream.
(A good, pleasant dream, one that you feel sad when you wake up and it ends.)
Then our mouth was filled with laughter,
(Did you see how Amy's little one tore around the tables?)
and our tongue with shouts of joy;
(I remember when my little ones had energy like that.)
then it was said among the nations,
(Let's change that to "Lincoln County, Kansas)
"The Lord has done great things for them."
(Could anyone not say we are richly blessed?)
The Lord has done great things for us, and we rejoiced.
("Rejoiced" means we felt joy again! It was like when the Sunday school was full and we had so many kids at Vacation Bible School!)
Restore our fortunes, O Lord, like the watercourses in the Negeb.
(Remind us of how we felt when the Dust Bowl finally passed.)
May those who sow in tears reap with shouts of joy.
(Lord, you can turn the worst moment in a person's life upside down because you love us so much!
Those who go out weeping,
(So many of our members were going to be lonely today...)
bearing the seed for sowing
shall come home with shouts of joy
carrying their sheaves.

Psalm 126:1-6 (NRSV).

(Their arms were filled with leftovers, and they had smiles on their faces when they walked upstairs.)

The psalm reminds us of the Lord's desire to destroy destruction and not merely to wipe our tears away, but to replace our tears with laughter.

The Lord knows we need to eat. Jesus said as much in this morning's lesson from the Sermon on the Mount.

Therefore I tell you, do not worry about your life, what you will eat or what you will drink, or about your body, what you will wear. Is not life more than food, and the body more than clothing? Look at the birds of the air; they neither sow nor reap nor gather into barns, and yet your heavenly Father feeds them. Are you not of more value than they?

Matthew 6:25-26 (NRSV).

One lesson the Presbyterians in Sylvan Grove, Kansas, relearned that Christmas afternoon was that one does not live by bread alone. Food is essential, they knew that, but people need more than food to be fully alive and healthy. The spirit of generosity and hospitality the Presbyterians discovered was renewing and invigorating for them in a way food alone could not have done.

They had hosted not a meal, but a feast! Feasts are so important in bringing people together, in nourishing our bodies and our souls. Food is simply fuel, but a feast feeds us with more than calories to keep our bodies going; feasts renew our spirits. The Presbyterians, and everyone else in Sylvan Grove, Kansas, had forgotten that part.

The prophet Joel knew how important feasts were. He could have been describing the scene in the basement of First Presbyterian Church in Sylvan Grove, Kansas, when he wrote:

You shall eat in plenty and be satisfied,
and praise the name of the Lord your God,
who has dealt wondrously with you.

Joel 2:26 (NRSV).

As we mark the national holiday that is Thanksgiving, let us never forget that it is from the Lord that all blessings flow. Let's eat!

Amen.

CPSIA information can be obtained
at www.ICGtesting.com
Printed in the USA
JSHW050607170920
7993JS00002B/120

9 780788 029998